Studying Social Networks

Marina Hennig is Professor for Social Network Research and Sociology of the Family at Johannes Gutenberg-Universität Mainz. *Ulrik Brandes* is Professor for Algorithmics in the Department of Computer and Information Science at the University of Konstanz. *Jürgen Pfeffer*, PhD is currently a Post-Doctoral Associate at the Center for Computational Analysis of Social and Organizational Systems (CASOS) at Carnegie Mellon University. *Ines Mergel* is an Assistant Professor of Public Administration and International Affairs at the Maxwell School of Citizenship and Public Affairs at Syracuse University.

Marina Hennig, Ulrik Brandes, Jürgen Pfeffer, Ines Mergel

Studying Social Networks

A Guide to Empirical Research

In collaboration with
Stephen P. Borgatti, Lothar Krempel, and Michael Schnegg

Campus Verlag
Frankfurt/New York

We gratefully acknowledge financial support from Deutsche Forschungsgemeinschaft (DFG) under grants He 5537/1-1 (Cooperation Network "Social Network Analysis") and Br 2158/6-1 (Reinhart Koselleck-Project "Social Network Algorithmics").

Bibliographic Information published by the Deutsche Nationalbibliothek.
The Deutsche Nationalbibliothek lists this publication in the Deutsche Nationalbibliografie; detailed bibliographic data are available in the Internet at http://dnb.d-nb.de.

Cover design: Guido Klütsch, Cologne
Printing office and bookbinder: CPI buchbuecher.de, Birkach
Printed on acid free paper.
Printed in Germany

This book is also available as an E-Book.
www.campus.de
www.press.uchicago.edu

Contents

Preface

Network paradigms are on the rise. Over the past two decades, they have diffused from sociology, anthropology, and social psychology into countless other disciplines. More and more phenomena are being conceptualized as networks because it appears that they are better suited to representing and explaining some complex dependencies that are not captured in population samples and feature vectors.

Accordingly, an increasing number of books about networks and network analysis is also being published. In our view, however, these are often centered on substantive problems addressed using network perspectives, on theoretical reflections about the role and function of networks, or on models and methodological contributions for the analysis of networks and complex systems in general. What appears to be missing is a textbook that builds on and updates the widely known and instantly classical texts by Wasserman and Faust (1994) and Scott (2000) but is more directly tailored to application in empirical studies.

The idea to put together an interdisciplinary group of researchers to address this apparent gap arose in a discussion between Marina Hennig and Ines Mergel during the Sunbelt XXVI Social Networks Conference (25–30 April 2006, Vancouver, BC). Steve Borgatti, Ulrik Brandes, Marina Hennig, Lothar Krempel, Ines Mergel, and Michael Schnegg then outlined a structure that would follow the empirical research process and include learning goals, examples, and exercises. This initial design was refined and implemented by the present authors. An important aspect of our approach is that we do not focus on networks in a specific domain or methods of a particular kind; instead, our intention is to provide a compact guide to the utilization of network approaches in the social sciences, in the broadest possible sense.

Many of these aspects have been shaped by the valuable feedback we received from participants in courses we have taught in various formats, disciplines, and locations. Additional input was provided by numerous colleagues and students within and outside of our working groups. We have also learned from each other, and sincerely hope that readers will feel that they benefit from this book as much as we did from the experience writing it.

Our heartfelt thanks go to everyone who has contributed to the completion of this project. The *Deutsche Forschungsgemeinschaft* (DFG) supported us financially with a Cooperation Network grant to Marina Hennig and a Reinhart Koselleck project grant to Ulrik Brandes. The Social Science Research Center Berlin provided administrative management support, and we are particularly grateful to Elisabeth Hamacher, Susanne Grasow, and Claudia Buchmann. We thank Susan Cox for copy-editing and Christine Agorastos for assistance in preparing the final manuscript. Jutta Allmendinger and Kathleen M. Carley provided much-appreciated guidance and support, and our own personal networks bore with us.

Berlin/Mainz, Konstanz,   *Marina Hennig*
Vienna/Pittsburgh, Syracuse   *Ulrik Brandes*
July 2012   *Jürgen Pfeffer*
                                                                  Ines Mergel

How to Use this Book

Each chapter starts with a paragraph like this stating the learning goals of the chapter. Its purpose is to provide a concise overview of what to expect in the subsequent sections.

In this very short chapter, you will learn about our reasons for organizing this book in the way we did and how we think you can get the most out of it. This includes suggestions for additional material such as software tools.

This book is written for students, researchers, and practitioners in all disciplines. It provides an introduction to the process of carrying out an empirical network study, assuming that you are familiar with – or familiarize yourself with by other means – the general principles of empirical research. In a nutshell, we roughly assume the following steps, possibly with iterations:

1. *Research question* (examples in Chapter 1)
2. *Substantive theory*
3. *Hypotheses*
4. Research design (Chapter 2)
5. Data collection (Chapter 3)
6. Exploration and analysis (Chapter 4)
7. *Interpretation* and presentation (Chapter 5)

A scientific paradigm is a combination of theories and corresponding methods. Since there can be no universal substantive network theory, the network approach is actually a family of paradigms which are mostly distinguished by their domain-specific theories. The items shown above in *italics* are specific to a domain and perspective, and not, therefore, covered in this book. For compactness, we also restrict the exposition to methods specific to network representations.

You are strongly encouraged to use one of the available software tools for network analysis to actively try out the concepts presented in this book. Some more widely used tools are: UCINET,[1] Pajek,[2] visone,[3,4] Tulip,[5] ORA,[6] NodeXL,[7] and the sna package[8] of R. Many more are listed in a dedicated Wikipedia article.[9] Some tools are accompanied by example data sets, and several collections of network data on the Internet provide realistic examples for reproduction and further analysis.[10]

Grey boxes separate additional material from the main text. These are often pointers to well-known network studies that we suggest for further reading. Following at least some of these pointers will give you a better understanding of the nature and scope of network studies. Instructors may find them useful in the compilation of seminar reading assignments.

Each chapter ends with a collection of exercises. Some are rather involved and require the extensive review of material presented in the chapter, and many are formulated as open-ended questions to encourage further self-study. Instructors may want to use them as inspiration for homework assignments or student projects.

Overall, our intention is to provide you with a frame of reference rather than a complete list of aspects and techniques. We hope that you find this book inspiring, and perhaps even fun. Enjoy!

---

1 http://www.analytictech.com/ucinet/
2 http://pajek.imfm.si/
3 http://www.visone.info/
4 Network diagrams in this book have been produced with visone.
5 http://tulip.labri.fr/
6 http://www.casos.cs.cmu.edu/projects/ora/
7 http://www.codeplex.com/nodexl/
8 http://erzuli.ss.uci.edu/R.stuff
9 http://en.wikipedia.org/wiki/Social_network_analysis_software
10 A good starting point which includes pointers to other repositories is Vladimir Batagelj's list at http://pajek.imfm.si/doku.php?id=data:index

1 Introduction

Social network studies entail the use of network representations to understand social phenomena. Social networks do not exist as such but only as concepts. This is illustrated by means of three example studies which also delineate the scope of this book.

Relations matter. You knew this, of course – Why else would you be interested in learning about social network analysis? The real questions are: How, where, when, and why do they matter? And, more pragmatically, how can you show that they do?

This book is organized along the process of an empirical study of social networks. It thus provides a guideline and orientation. While we concentrate on the things that are not treated in textbooks on empirical studies of population samples (i.e., non-relational studies), we still think that the book is largely self-contained.

So, what is the subject of a network study?

1.1 The Construction of Social Networks

It has become commonplace to refer to interacting or otherwise dependent entities as networks. The phenomena described as networks range from the social interactions of human beings and the flow of goods between countries to gene regulation and railroad infrastructures. What do these examples have in common that leads us to think we can model and analyze them in similar ways?

Some of the phenomena referred to as networks are real in the sense that their existence does not depend on our perspective. Online social networking services, for example, are technology-enabled products. As such they have well-defined elements. A friending protocol specifies the sequences of actions that yield a link between two user accounts. The immanent meaning of such a link is unambiguous. We may refer to the web of linked accounts as a network or not, in any case, it is represented in the service provider's databases.

However, the social network of human beings who own accounts in the above system is an inferred, construed object. It has no independent existence and is thus always subject to interpretation. In these cases, the use of the term network is that of a model or metaphor; it does not denote an unambiguous object but a perspective.

As a metaphor the term "network" is very graphic, immediately evoking images of points and connecting line segments.[1] Metaphors are very useful for memorization and creative thinking. However, it is not necessarily obvious which aspects of a metaphor correspond to actual properties of that which is represented, and which aspects do not.

Another pitfall of metaphors and models alike is the use of similar representations for weakly related phenomena. By abstracting from the nonessential (with respect to a specific perspective), otherwise invalid commonalities and conclusions may emerge. To illustrate this point, consider (statistical) "distributions" as another example of a representation. If both the distribution of life-expectancy in the east of Austria and the household income in a suburb of Berlin are unimodal (i.e., have a single peak), does this imply that there is a relation between these two phenomena? We assume that you would not think so, but it appears to be much more tempting to speculate about such relations when two networks exhibit similar features because it is more easily forgotten that they are simplifying and homogenizing, reductionist representations.

The study of social networks is, hence, the study of a particular type of representation in social science contexts (Freeman 1989). Therefore, social networks are constructs and do not exist as such. They are representations, in which aspects of a social phenomenon – aspects that seem to be relevant in a specific context and for a specific purpose – are expressed in ways more amenable to scientific scrutiny.

Since there are no social networks per se, it is a linguistic simplification when we say that we are studying social networks. In fact we are studying social phenomena by means of network representations. This is carried

---

1 It appears that the term "social network" was coined in Barnes (1954), in which precisely this image is evoked.

out by gathering data about aspects of a phenomenon and organizing the data in a convenient form, by applying methods that produce additional, derived data, and translating these back to the realm of the phenomenon. Clearly, this is no different from other empirical investigations. What is distinct in network analysis, however, are the kinds of data and methods, and the reasoning that motivates network representations and justifies the interpretation of results.

1.2 Social Network Studies

We consider an empirical investigation a network study, if the underlying theory, the data, or both, focus on pair-wise relationships. Hence, the commonalities of network studies lie not so much in the phenomena under scrutiny but in the conceptual focus on relations. The following three examples illustrate this position and many other studies are outlined in grey boxes throughout this book.

1.2.1 The Community Question (Wellman 1979)

The growth of cities and the associated modernization processes constitute an important topic in urban sociology research. Community sociology-based urban research, in particular, often described processes of change as loss events: loss of familiarity, belonging, neighborhood, community, and small social networks. Within this tradition of community research, "urbanism" per se is equated with the development towards an "anonymous mass society" (cf. Wirth's classical essay of 1938).

In the course of urban modernization processes (for example, in the form of urban rehabilitation projects) and the associated residential mobility, the majority of affected residents experienced loss and grief reactions of varying intensity, which were explained in terms of the loss of spatial identity and the networks of relationships that had developed over generations (Fried 1963; and summary in Mühlich, Zinn, Kröning, and Mühlich-Klinger 1978).

The lament over "community lost," which has been a fundamental theme of social scientific urban research (cf. Wellman and Leighton 1979) since the 1930s, is combined here with an excessive romantic elevation of the patterns that have disappeared. As a counter thesis to the loss of

community the assumption emerged that neighborhood and family solidarity continues to exist in developed industrial-bureaucratic social systems. This position, which is known as the "saved argument," asserts
that, due to its ongoing effectiveness, community solidarity lives on in
the provision of support and sociability and the community demand for
informal social control and environmentally-friendly integration into ho-
mogeneous residential areas and places of work. The saved argument attained a new orthodoxy in the 1960s through the publication of studies
such as "Urban Village" (Gans 1962), Greer's (1962) theoretical development of post-war survey research, and Jacobs' (1961) comments on the
vitality of the density of diverse city centers.

Whereas the culturally pessimistic line in the interpretation of urban
processes of change laments the disintegration of a positive attitude to
life – or "sense of community" in the sense used by Sarason (1974) and
Glynn (1981) – an opposing pattern of interpretation sees the opportunity for and beginning of a "community liberated" in the disintegration
of life forms dictated by tradition: The overcoming of cramped conditions and density, which contain both ties and social control, represents
an important precondition for the individualization of persons. They
gain the possibility of associating with people of their own choice, freeing
themselves from rigid status allocations, and entering into and organizing relationships in accordance with their own voluntary needs. In the
loose relationship ties that can be terminated at any time, scope for action arises that is characteristic of the urban subject. Most commentators,
who participated in the "community" debate using the "lost," "saved," and
"liberated" arguments viewed this as something akin to an alternative description of the "reality" of contemporary life, or the developmental suc-
cession from the pre-industrial saved community to the lost community,
which was replaced, in turn, by the post-industrial liberated community
(Wellman, Carrington, and Hall 1988: 135).

In the course of the many community analyses carried out, however,
the fundamental structural concern about the question of community was
often transformed into a search for local solidarity instead of one focusing
on functioning primary relationships. It was assumed a priori here that
a significant proportion of urban primary relationships are organized locally. Hence, Wellman (1979) suggests that the community question be
studied from a network-analytic perspective. The benefit of the network
perspective consists in the fact that it does not take supposed – local or
kinship – solidarities as its starting point and does not aim primarily to

find and explain the persistence of feelings of solidarity. Instead, it is interested in presenting the structure of relationships and flow of activities so that the focus in the community debate is no longer on normative and spatial preferences but on the fundamental structural issues raised by the community question.

To this end, the question as to the effects of the differentiated social structure of the macro level on the significant social connections and relationships between individuals on the micro level is reformulated. For Wellman, social integration is not the community that is integrated via normative orientations but an integration achieved through the nature of the relationship structures. Forms of solidarity communities that can be closely defined spatially are no longer sought but, instead, strong relationships that are not characterized by spatial delineation but by their integrating function. Wellman et al. (1988) formulated the theoretical positions from community research in three theories – community lost, community saved, and community liberated – and applied the forms of the structural characteristics fostered as ideal types (see Figure 1) for an ego-centered network analysis and analyzed them in an empirical study on East York.

In 1968, Coates and Wellman surveyed 845 ego-centered networks in the Toronto neighborhood of East York (Wellman 1993: 426). A name generator was used for the purpose: "I'd like to ask you a few questions about the people outside your home that you feel closest to; these could be friends, neighbors or relatives." (Wellman 1979: 1209)

Of the named alteri, only the first six were recorded and taken into account for the remainder of the survey. Ego was then asked whether the named alteri had the same relationship with each other, i.e., whether they were close to each other. The role of the alteri for ego, the alteri's gender, the nature and frequency of contact between them (i.e., telephone, letter, or face-to-face), place of residence and distance between alter's and ego's residences, and the guaranteeing of everyday and emergency assistance from the alteri were also surveyed (Wellman 1979; Wellman, Carven, Whitaker, Stevens, Shorter, DuTroit, and Bakker 1973; Wellman and Hiscott 1985). An example is shown in Figure 2.

Wellmann found hardly any network structures in his East York study that could be clearly classified in accordance with the "lost" theory. The surveyed networks tended to correspond to the forms of the other two theories, however they could not easily be classified. Most of the networks displayed elements of both theories. In addition to these find-

community characteristics	lost	saved	liberated
size of networks	very small	very large	large
origins	friends, organizations	kin, neighborhood	friends, workplace
duration	short	long	mostly short
roles	acquaintances	kin, neighbors	friends, co-workers
socio-physical context	public, private	communal spaces	private spaces
residential separation	somewhat dispersed	local	highly dispersed
frequency of contact	low	high (much in person)	high (much phone use)
structural embeddedness	none	very high	high
network context	low	large group	small clusters
density	very low	very high	moderate overall, with dense clusters
cluster overlap	dyads	one big cluster,	low
number of network pieces (components+ isolates)	many small fragments and isolates	one big cluster, no isolates	several small clusters and isolates
cluster dominance	no	yes, by one	yes, by several
abundance of aid	low	high	moderate
variety of aid	low	high	high
articulation with large-scale social systems	little (companionship only)	defensive coping with demands companionship	ways of accessing resources, companionship
specialization	specialized ties	multistranded ties	specialized ties
reciprocity	low, only dyadic	high, communal	high, within circles

Figure 1: Ideal types of ego-centered networks according to Wellman, Carrington, and Hall (1988: 130–184).

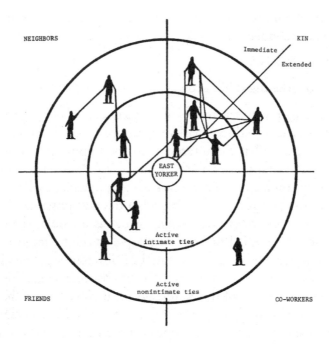

Figure 2: Personal network of an East Yorker (reproduced from Wellman and Berkowitz 1988: 27).

ings, what is interesting about Wellman's study is his reconceptualization of the community question, which was initially formulated in macro-sociological terms, in network-analytic terms with a view to making it applicable to a micro-sociological study (cf. Diaz-Bone 1997: 156). Wellman's use of ego-centered networks here reflects personal, experienceable circumstances of the micro level that can arise simultaneously in a society, which can be used in the description of the macro structure by generalizing them (cf. Diaz-Bone 1997: 156). With Wellman's help, this can be used to demonstrate the personal networks of important relationships (cf. Wellman 1979; Wellman et al. 1988).

This example clearly demonstrates how network analysis provides the basis for a discourse on the effects of societal modernization on the individual, the development of familiar life forms, and social relationships, and shows that, although one model or another can dominate in a social system, it is more likely that all three models are present in current reality, at least in part. This means that a personal community can consist of a mixture of close-knit core clusters and a few lose-knit relationships, which also have connections with other groups and their resources.

1.2.2   Viral Marketing (Hill, Provost, and Volinsky 2006)

Hill et al. (2006) presents the results of a *network-based marketing* study. It analyzes the impact of a direct marketing campaign on different customer segments. In particular, the interest is in the importance of consumer networks for the adoption of a new product. In 2004, a telecommunications company conducted a direct-marketing campaign to sell a new "high tech" service to their customers. To obtain the best possible success rate by keeping the costs of the campaign as low as possible, the company decided to select a limited number of people as the target group of the marketing efforts. The company created 21 different segments based on demographic attributes and history with the costumers (e.g., loyalty). In addition to the segments of the company, the involved researchers added a second dimension to grouping the costumers—whether a person was directly connected through its telephone communications network to people that already used the particular new service or not. Consequently, the customers were separated for the analysis into four groups.

1. Traditionally selected customers that were not embedded in networks with existing users.
2. People that were selected twice via the traditional targeting of the company and based on the network connections to existing users.
3. People that were not part of the 21 segments but were selected by the company as, despite failing to provide demographic and historic evidence for becoming a customer of the new service, they had network connections to at least one existing user.
4. People that were not part of the marketing campaign at all but were connected to existing users.

Not very surprisingly, the second group had the highest take rates for the new service (1.25 percent). The following results were more unexpected—for the telecommunications company's marketing staff, at least. The take rate of the third group of people, which was not profiled as possible purchasers of the product but had connections to existing customers, was three times higher than that of the first group of traditionally selected people who were not connected to existing users of the service (0.83 percent and 0.28 percent). Moreover, the third group outperformed every one of the 21 different segments that were selected on the basis of different demographic and historic attributes. Another impressive finding was made by the authors when they looked at the fourth group of non-targeted people who had connections with existing customers. The take rate for this group was 0.11 percent. Hill et al. (2006: 269) state that "although they were not even marketed to, their take rate is almost half that for the non-NN [non-network neighbor] targets." In addition, this is about ten times higher than the estimated 0.01 percent take rate for non-targeted people who were not connected to existing customers. In summary, Hill et al. (2006) presents convincing reasoning for the fact that when it comes to the proliferation of new products, connections to existing customers are significantly more important for successful adoption than any demographic attribute or any preceding relationships between company and customers.

1.2.3 Corporate Networks (Windolf 2006)

Until the last third of the 19th century, the family was a central institution in the coordination of transactions and mobilization of resources. Company management consisted predominantly of family members and the family often acted as lender of last resort. With the emergence of large companies, the familial organizational framework was exceeded. Complex transactions could no longer be controlled through familial relationships. Together with the large corporations, the network emerged as a new institution that facilitated the coordination of transactions, the supervision of management, and the social integration of the economic elite.

The network became a cross-company coordination instrument that increasingly superseded the family group. It largely freed itself from its ascriptive characteristics (family and ownership), and it became increasingly professionalized (professional supervisory board, management studies) and subject to regulation. The network constitutes an important element of this modernization process, in the course of which late 19th century capitalism was organized or rationalized.

The analyses of company networks in organized capitalism in Germany and the USA in the period from 1896 to 1938 focus on two functions which are fulfilled by the network and show that an opportunity structure was created through the network that made it possible to pursue different interests. These include the supervision function, on the one hand, and the regulation of competition, on the other.

Control Function

The relationship between the owners and managers in big corporations with thousands of shareholders is hampered by a principal-agent problem: managers have more information and competence. Hence the monitoring of managers became a central problem for corporations.

The function for controlling ownership was replaced by the social control in peer groups. The mutual presence of top managers in the supervisory bodies may be understood as a declaration that the company complies with business ethical standards and the shareholder is not being deceived.

The network provides social infrastructure, in the context of which the compliance with standards can be monitored. In this sense, the members produce a public good, the network's moral capital.

The company network is part of a comprehensive coordination and control system, to which large industrial concerns, universal banks and interest groups belong. Rudolf Hilferding coined the term "organized capitalism" to describe this institutional system. Organized capitalism is based on predictability, continuous profit yields, the bureaucratization of large companies, and the replacement of charismatic entrepreneurship by academically trained management.

Only when economic transactions are rationalized in this way can banks guarantee the reliable and continuous financing of large companies and capital-intensive mass production.

Whereas the banks in the USA provided loans, the banks in Germany were direct shareholders in companies.

Regulating the Competition

Companies that compete in a market make greater profits if they coordinate their behavior with each other.

Two different forms of coordination emerged in the USA and Germany, namely the trust and the cartel. The cartel is federal in structure: Member companies retain their legal and economic independence. Collective control prevents an individual company from gaining a monopoly. Price is often dictated by the weaker members of a group. The trust tends to lead to a centralized monopoly under uniform leadership. The member companies relinquish not only their economic independence but also their legal autonomy. Competition is not regulated in the trust but tends to be eliminated.

While developments in Germany were characterized by cartels, in the USA, increasing monopolization through the emergence of trusts led to anti-trust laws (Sherman Act).

The competition market is not a spontaneous, self-regulating institution; it must be repeatedly reconstructed through continuous control and state intervention.

In contrast, the model of regulated competition is regulated corporatistically. It does not propagate state control but the autonomous control of the market participants in an interest group. In this context, the company network is an institution that is complementary to the cartel. It strengthened the integration of the cartel members through their mutual presence on the supervisory boards. During the lifetime of a cartel agreement, conflicts of interests can be resolved and contractual adaptations be negotiated in the network.

The data records used in Windolf (2006) for Germany and the USA for the period from 1896 to 1938 contain a total of almost 40,000 relationships (interlocks), collected from a multitude of historical data sources.

The focus of interest here was the mandates of the supervisory boards in the different countries and the intersectoral networks, i.e., the question as to how strongly different economic sectors are networked. These data were compared either at national level over time (does the density increase or decrease?) or between the countries over time.

The data originate from a total survey of large companies in the year in question. The analyses relate only to this group of companies. The network border is defined relatively arbitrarily by the list of large companies. The network extends beyond the big companies, however, for example to small private banks and family enterprises. These relationships were not recorded in the study under discussion here. The analyses were not concentrated on the interests that were actually pursued by different actors in the network but on the opportunity structures that arise through the network. Hence the network offers the opportunity to stabilize the cooperation between rational egoists; it offers the chance to exercise control within a networked peer group and to sanction the contravention of business ethics principles. The more comprehensive the network and the greater the density, the greater the chances of achieving cooperation based on universal performance criteria in the network.

Certain assumptions about the structure of the network were extrapolated from the above-presented theoretical considerations. For example: If banks were an important supervisory body, it would have to be proven that they assumed a central position in the network (actor degree centrality). And if the German banks had a strong interest in supervision due to their involvement in the granting of credit, they should be represented in (relatively) more companies as compared with the U.S. banks. The structural characteristics examined include multiple relationships, density, centrality and degree of the overall network and individual components.

The result of the analyses showed that the network in Germany developed into a coordination instrument that facilitated the cooperation between large companies. From 1928, fewer than ten per cent of the companies were isolated/marginal. This proportion was considerably higher in the USA (approximately 27 percent in 1928). From 1914 on, relationships per company and multiple relationships (redundancy) were considerably higher in Germany. The higher the redundancy, the greater the network density. The stronger centralization of German network can be interpreted as indicating higher supervision intensity. It was also shown that, in Germany, not only the banks had many contacts but also the industrial concerns. As opposed to this, in the USA, the finance companies were the most central actors. Hence, in Germany, not only the supervision of the banks but also the coordination of market processes were an important function of the network. The decline in the relationships in Germany between 1928 and 1938 can be explained by the legal regulation, on the one hand, and the liquidation of key Jewish companies/banks, on the other. In addition, it was possible to show that the intersectoral network in Germany was relatively high and increased continuously between 1896 and 1938. Therefore the network was used – in parallel to the cartels – as an instrument for the coordination of the market (regulated competition). The relatively high intersectoral networking in Germany between some economic sectors of heavy industry (coal, steel, chemistry, mechanical engineering) indicates that the network was used as a substitute for vertical integration or as a precursor of a vertical concern. The German banks were relatively strongly networked with the heavy industry sectors, but – in comparison to other economic sectors – they did not have the highest average network density. Before the First World War, the structure of intrasectoral/intersectoral networking between Germany and the USA was relatively similar. The two countries developed differently thereafter: Whereas intrasectoral networking declined in the USA, it increased in Germany.

In summary, the study shows that the networking between large corporations was an important element in the system of economic institutions, which developed in late 19th century and provided a solution for specific problems associated with emerging organized capitalism. In the large corporations, the control of ownership was replaced by the alternating control of managers in the supervisory board or board of directors. The empirical structural analysis has shown that the network could be used as an efficient control instrument, particularly in Germany.

The network was also a supervision instrument for the banks, which took a considerable risk by granting investment loans, and associated their existence with the "long-term fate" of the industrial concern. In Germany, in particular, the network alleviated the problem of debtor opportunism. Until 1928, the proportion of large companies, in which a banker was represented on the supervisory board, increased to over 50 percent; this percentage was only slightly lower in the USA. The analysis also showed that the banks did not control the industrial concerns. The banks were lenders (Germany) or financial intermediaries (USA), and in this capacity forced the companies to adopt rational company management practices. The banks were important actors in the process of the rationalization of capitalism. In the age of early mass production and constantly increasing capital intensity (fixed costs), uncontrolled competition between the large companies was dysfunctional. The network provided an institutional framework, in which market processes could be coordinated and competition could be regulated.

1.3   Exercises

1. Collect definitions of "social network" and "social network analysis" from the literature. How are social networks, underlying theories, and means of analysis distinguished from other paradigms? How do these definitions apply to the above three example studies?
2. Network ties can both facilitate and constrain the actions of social actors. How do the interdependencies in social networks differ from those in markets or hierarchies as more restricted forms of organization?
3. Read the original references and compare at least two of the above example studies with respect to the following questions:

   - What is the overall research question?

- What precisely constitutes the networks of interest? Which data are collected and analyzed?

- Why are these networks relevant for the research question, i.e., what makes relationships between actors essential? How is this argued for?

- How does the particular structure, evolution, or functioning of networks enter the conclusions?

4. Write down at least twelve distinct relations that may exist between individuals, organizations, or animals. Try to classify them according to any characteristic. Discuss for which type of research question they may be relevant, and why monadic attribute data is insufficient for that purpose.

2 Research Design

The aim of this chapter is to provide an introduction to different research designs and to assist you in developing a design for your own project. A research design links the research question to data collection techniques (including sampling) and, eventually, data analysis. There is no standardized way of carrying out a network study. This means that there is no "one size fits it all" solution to a research problem involving networks. There are two sides to this coin. It is a disadvantage, on the one hand, as it requires more planning and thinking on your part. On the other hand, however, it offers you a tremendous opportunity. It makes the research process a very creative exercise that can and must develop a strategy specifically tailored to your problem. In order to assist you in developing such a research design, this chapter will: (i) introduce you to various widely known approaches; and (ii) assist you in formulating and focusing on your research question. This enables you to determine which technique – or combination of techniques – may be best suited to address your research problem.

The previous chapter introduced you to the kinds of questions network researchers ask. The common denominator of these questions is the key role played by social relationships. Both the questions and the information required to answer them differ from more common survey research. Typically, at least three things are required for the development of a research design: the definition of the units of analysis, the decision as to how to select them, and the selection of the variables or attributes to be collected for each unit of analysis. Units of analysis are the social entities whose behavior we wish to describe and explain. These may be individuals, households, communities, firms, nation states, etc.

Throughout this book we reserve the term variable to refer to a characteristic of a single actor or tie, and refer to all variables of the same characteristic as an attribute. Attributes can as diverse as the actors' gender, political orientation, or personal goals. Please note that attributes can vary in terms of their complexity. While gender can be captured as a one-dimensional concept (male, female), a concept like political orientation usually involves more than one dimension (e.g., attitudes towards the death penalty, war on terror, abortion, etc). Goals and individual strategies are even more complex and can often best be captured using less structured qualitative data. Survey research relies on these attributes to answer questions such as whether political orientation differs between people of different gender or age.

Network research takes the social context into account. Network studies rely on more than data about actors and their attributes, they also require information about the way in which the actors are related, i.e., their social ties. The study of social networks is based on the reasoning that seemingly autonomous individuals and organizations are, in fact, embedded in social relations and interactions (Borgatti, Mehra, Brass, and Labianca 2009). The term "social network" sets this decidedly structuralist perspective apart from other research traditions focusing on social groups and social categories (Barnes 1954).

The basic entities of network analysis are dyads. A dyad consists of a pair of actors and is used to identify the variables associated with relationships between specific actors. Actors are part of multiple dyads because relationships can potentially exist with several other actors. Network analysis therefore differs from dyadic data analysis of unrelated dyads (Kenny, Kashy, and Cook 2006). Typical actors include, for example, people in a group, departments of a company, and countries. These are linked through social relationships that differ in terms of their content, direction, and intensity. Examples of relationships include personal relationships (friendship, respect, etc.), affiliations (to associations, departments, etc.), formal power relations (authority, etc.), and physical connections.

Sociological network analysis looks at individual and at collective actors (e.g., companies) not as "social islands," (Flap 2002) which are characterized mainly by a number of specific features, but as agents who interact with other players and are influenced by these patterns of interaction. In contrast with conventional statistical procedures, the focus of interest in network analysis is not, therefore, on the attributes of actors but their relationships and the structures and functions of interpersonal and organizational networks.

Which relationships are examined depends, of course, largely on the research question. under investigation. The simplest question concerning a relationship determines only whether a relationship exists or not. More differentiated questions look at the intensity of a relationship. In such cases an intensity scale is needed to describe the relation, which is referred then to as a valued relationship. In the case of the question "Who visited whom at home?," for example, the relationship intensity can vary significantly. Person i may come to see person j several times a week, while person j has visited person i only once in the past year. Hence, it is obvious that an intensity scale needs to be created for the visit rate per unit of time. However, it is also immediately apparent that somebody who has belonged to the network under examination for a few days only will hardly have had the possibility to build up a visit network. Therefore, the duration of membership in the network can influence an actor's pattern of visit relationships. A special type of relationship arises when the definition of the relationship refers to certain events. Possible examples of such events would be the meeting of an association or a garden party. In this case, you record who participates in such an event with whom (through observation, questioning the participant, or reviewing documents). The relationships between actors are, therefore, reconstructed on the basis of their joint participation in events.

2.1 Social Networks

"A social network consists of a finite set or sets of actors and the relation or relations defined on them." (Wasserman and Faust 1994: 20)

Pair-wise relations defined on a set of actors correspond to relationships defined on a set of dyads. These dyads constitute a larger structure which describes the social network. The key assumption is that the overlapping structure of network dyads results in interdependencies among relationships.

Explicitly or implicitly, social networks often play the role of intermediate meso-level variables, which moderate the effect of antecedents, such as individual behavior, on consequences such as collective action, possibly with feedback.

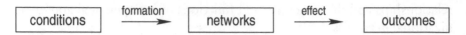

Figure 3: Networks as explanatory, dependent, or intermediary variables.

Therefore, a crucial distinction for network-based research in any domain is that between a *theory of networks* of a certain type (e.g., What is the nature of specific relations, what are the constituents of an emergent structure, how can these be measured?) and a *network theory* of the domain which informs the analysis (e.g., How do the structural characteristics of relations affect other variables?). For convenience we refer to the former as a theory of networks (network antecedents) and the latter as network theory of consequences of network structure.

The research questions posed in a network-analytical approach follow the basic understanding that network observations are not independent. We try to understand how network actors are connected to each other and hence influence each other's behavior (*connectionist view*), and how their interactions influence the overall network structure (*structuralist view*). Based on this view we can distinguish two different types of network analysis research questions:

– Why and how do network actors interact with each other in the observed way (network antecedents)?
– What are the consequences of the observed network structure, such as performance, extent of resource sharing, etc. (consequences of network structure)?

The network causality chain is shown in Figure 3.

Examples of research questions that use antecedents to explain the observed network structure include studies which examine the influence of human capital on the creation of social capital. In this example, the network structures and properties are the dependent variable and the theory of networks concerns the antecedents of network phenomena. Typical research questions that explain the influence of the social structure on a specific consequence include, for example: How does networking across organizational boundaries affect team effectiveness? (Joshi 2006) How does the centrality of an organizational unit affect its performance? (Tsai 2001) How do social interactions affect trust in product innovations? (Tsai and Ghoshal 1998) For these questions the network structure is the explanatory variable and the theory concerns the consequences of network phenomena—i.e., how network processes and mechanisms lead to certain outcomes for individual nodes or entire networks.

Moreover, it is possible to identify examples, such as Burt's study on the creation of so-called *structural holes* and their influence on the creation of ideas (Burt 2004),[1] in which both antecedents and consequences of network structure are included in one and the same study.

2.2 Networks as Variables

As indicated in the introduction, network analysis advances prevailing empirical social research in a way that enables not only the characteristics of individuals such as age, gender, or status to be the subject of analysis, but also the ways in which individuals act in different contexts and the roles in which they are embedded in the surrounding social environment. The network concept achieves a level of theoretical openness here which is suitable for recording and demonstrating empirically the action spaces and relationship work that develop alongside the institutionalized world and reproduce social reality. The real subject of network analysis is the relationship structure. The relationship structure is considered here as an explanatory fact for social action and social phenomena. Network analysis can be identified as an interdisciplinary paradigm of a number of social sciences that is characterized by a degree of formalization and has significantly expanded the field of social science. Instead of examining individual characteristics, the concept of social structure is not only used symbolically but is also described and analyzed.

The study of Wellman (1979) summarized in Section 1.2.1 provides an example of a largely descriptive project. However, his research question was theoretically driven. He took up an old and controversial debate in urban sociology, i.e., that concerning the effects of urbanization on community organization. Pessimistic social theorists (Wirth 1938) had argued that the social fabric would break down in the emerging cities. Others, including Gans (1962) for example, observed the "Little Italies" and "Little Chinatowns" which extended social and cultural systems to the emerging metropolitan areas.

---

1 Burt defined structural holes as missing relations between different components within a network that can produce a loss of information or an imbalance.

Box 1: Moreno's Refugees

During World War II, Jacob L. Moreno worked as a medical officer in a refugee camp in Mittendorf, south of Vienna. More than 10,000 mainly elderly people, women, and children from a South Tyrolean vineyard lived in this camp. They were stationed in Mittendorf to protect them against the Italian army. On the surface, the camp appeared to be well organized. There were community facilities and a shoe factory for 2,000 workers was moved to the camp to create employment opportunities. However, this well-intentioned step caused considerable tension. The people from the shoe factory believed themselves to be better than the rural refugees. "Another social layer was placed over the original refugees," observed Moreno (1995: 69). He became increasingly interested in the feelings and social tensions between peasants and workers, staff and refugees, men and women. He diagnosed these tensions as the main source of disturbances in camp life. He regretted that social and psychological issues were not considered in the planning of the camp. Moreno wrote a letter to the Austria-Hungarian Ministry of Interior stating: "The positive and negative feelings within each house and between the houses, within the factory and between the different religious, national, and political groups of the camp can be demonstrated through a sociometric analysis of the relations that prevail among the residents. A reorganization using sociometric methods is enclosed." (Moreno 1916 in Moreno 1953) Hence, he proposed that the camp be reorganized using sociometric methods. His plan was backed by the experience that "the families tended to help each other if people could live alongside those to whom they felt drawn in positive way." (Moreno 1953: 71)

Network diagrams offer another very intuitive way of describing social configurations. They show the overall shape of the network, however they also incorporate the risk that the layout will give rise to misinterpretations. While diagrams enable the communication of some of the basic properties of the network, more specialized numerical techniques are often better suited to comparing the positions of actors within an image and between two or more groups.

In one of the first sociological studies of community organization (see Box 2, Lundberg combined two approaches to offer a new perspective on

Box 2: Lundberg's Village Community

George A. Lundberg analyzed the entire social structure of a small village community (population around 1,000) in Vermont, USA. Of the 272 members of the community, 256 were interviewed about their closest friends within the community. In addition to the information about friendships within the community, visiting patterns and correspondence with the outside world were also recorded. To understand the patterns that emerged from these relationships, attributes like age, occupation, and economic and family status were measured using both single-item and more complex scales (e.g., Chapin scale designed for the measurement of socio-economic status). Lundberg analyzed these data so as to: (i) identify different social configurations ("nuclei" in his terminology), including stars, and isolate the most important patterns; and (ii) explain which members of the community held more central positions than others. The most frequently cited example from his research is the famous *Lady Bountiful*," a rich 60-year-old lady who was generous in her donations to the community and was named by 17 people in the community while she herself named only one relationship—a physician and politician who did not reciprocate the tie (Lundberg and Lawsing 1937; Lundberg and Steele 1938).

what he had identified as the central theme in sociology: social groupings.[2] He had already argued in the 1930s that social groupings were theorized in the past as interactions between conscious groups (e.g., classes).[3] He aimed to overcome this categorical approach by focussing on social linkages that were the focus of art and not science. Lundberg summarized that "The present paper is mainly concerned with the problem of representing more objectively some of these community nuclei which are at present considered the subtler and more intangible facts of community

---

2 A social group consists of two or more people who interact with one another and who recognize themselves as a distinct social unit. The definition is simple enough, but it has significant implications. Frequent interaction leads people to share values and beliefs. This similarity and the interaction cause them to identify with one another. Identification and attachment, in turn, stimulate more frequent and intense interaction.

3 A very interesting analysis of this relationship is White (2008).

structure, and which have hitherto, therefore, been left chiefly to literary and philosophic exploitation." (Lundberg and Lawsing 1937: 323)

Both of these case studies show how relatively simple network measures and graphical representations can be used to describe social phenomena (see Chapter 5). Network descriptions offer new insights into relatively unknown phenomena and populations (Lundberg) and enable the testing of different theoretical predictions about the social world (Wellman). In most network research projects an initial exploratory phase is followed by attempts to explain the causes of certain social configurations and what they, in turn, give rise to.

While all network theories emphasize the link between the two phenomena – network structure and behavior – they differ in terms of the ways in which they specify the causal relationship. Let us consider an example: If we wish to explain how gang membership and deviant behavior among inner city youths are related, the answer may lead in two directions: (i) Deviant behavior explains the kind of people with whom an individual hangs out; or (ii) the people with whom an individual hangs out explains whether or not they are likely to break the law. In the first case, deviant behavior is assumed to be the cause, in the latter it is assumed to be the consequence. In reality, the relationship is likely to be more complex and involve structural factors such as the neighborhood context, family background, and other variables that circumscribe both gang membership and behavior. Most researchers agree that the solution to the problem has two sides: i.e., empirical and theoretical. Empirically, the problem can only be solved using data collected over a period of time (longitudinal) which enables the identification of the temporal order between cause and consequence. However, the temporal order is not enough if we lack a theoretical model that describes the relationship between the two phenomena (Carley 1999).

Analyzing the evolution of social structure and behavior simultaneously poses an enormous theoretical and empirical challenge and very few studies have succeeded in accomplishing this goal (Steglich, Snijders, and Pearson 2010).

In the process of developing a research design for your project, this theoretical question translates to the issue that you would like to explain. Therefore, the central question for the research design is what we would like to explain in context of the network. Is the point of interest the question as to why people are linked in a specific way or do we want to explain how social relationships influence behavior? In practical terms, the first decision you will have to make in analyzing your research question is whether social networks constitute the explanatory or the dependent variable.

2.2.1 Explanatory Variables

In cases in which, the network is the explanatory variable, the effects of network integration should be explained by the behavior of individuals or groups. This is based on the assumption that integration into social networks affects behavior. Mark Granovetter's embeddedness theory provides a well-known explanation of this phenomenon (Granovetter 1985). Granovetter assumes that actors are not led by narrowly defined self-interests in their actions but take social contexts into account. Such contexts also relativize the orientations towards role regulations and norms and the meaning of higher institutional regulations like market and hierarchy.

In other words: The specific qualities of a network influence the behavior. For instance, the composition of a network can be of relevance to the division of labor in households (see Box 3).

Bott (1964) localized the network between the family and the environment. It marks the immediate social environment of a family and should not be confused with the formal institutions or organizations, however the environment constrains the configuration of the network. This consideration goes back to Peter Blau, who was the first to allocate a space, the so-called *Blau space*, to a wide variety of social forces. Blau (1977) conceptualizes the structure as a quantitative distribution of social positions that influence the interaction and role relationships (acting role) of people. For Blau, social structure is a multidimensional space of social positions, in which resources such as age, sex, education, income, etc. are distributed. These social forces structure the action of the actors. Thus, the personality of couples and the complex environmental factors such as professional positions, education, formal institutions, mobility, etc. also influence the variations in the network density.

To summarize: In cases, in which a network can be defined as the independent variable, the question is how the network structure influences the action or behavior of the embedded elements.

Box 3: Bott's Families

Elizabeth Bott (1964) was the first researcher to use personal network characteristics to explain behavior. She was interested in examining the relationship between network structure and conjugal role relationships among 20 lower and middle-class families in London.

In her study, conjugal role relationships were classified according to the extent to which both partners shared tasks and activities, ranging from the organization of work in the household to leisure activities. Based on a number of quantitative and qualitative instruments, she classified activities as being carried out *complementarily*, *independently*, and *jointly*. To learn about the structure of the networks, she used a fixed roster of questions which she asked all informants in a semi-structured interview.

The evaluation of the network relationships with relatives, neighbors, friends, and colleagues provided a connection between conjugal role behavior and the degree of network connectivity. This meant that the networks between those who had clear tasks were particularly close. In contrast, when tasks were accomplished jointly, the networks were more loose-knit (see Bott 1964: 59ff). Between these two extremes, however, there were "many degrees of variation" (Bott 1964: 59). The close-knit networks were found in particular among couples who lived in the environment in which they had grown up after the marriage. The more often the couples moved, the more likely the relationships in the networks were to be loose-knit. Hence, Bott arrived at the following central thesis: "The degree of segregation in the role-relationship of husband and wife varies directly with the connectedness of the family's social network." (Bott 1964: 60)

This means that "The more connected the network, the greater the degree of segregation between roles of husband and wife. The less connected the network, the smaller the degree of segregation between the roles of husband and wife" (see above). Therefore, for Bott, the connectedness of networks was the central attribute for describing the connections between the local environment and the division of labor between husband and wife. Moreover, she makes a distinction between "close-knit" and "loose-knit" (Bott 1964: 59) relations. The difference between the two types consists in the network composition of the married couples. In a "close-knit" network, the main contacts are with friends, neighbors, and relatives, and everyone in the network knows all of the other actors. In "loose-knit" networks, there are fewer friends, neighbors, and relatives. In addition, the alteri do not know all the other actors in the network.

2.2.2 Dependent Variables

If social networks are the dependent variable, we would like to show and explain why people are linked in a specific way. This usually involves two steps: i.e., (i) the description of the patterns of social organization; and (ii) the explanation of differences at the individual or the group level. At the individual level, we may be interested in finding out how linkages are distributed and whether all actors are equally popular. At the group level, we may want to know whether and how the group is divided into different disconnected components. Both descriptions lead to variables that describe the structural position of an individual, e.g., the number of times he or she was chosen, or the cluster, to which he or she belongs.

The explanation of network ties is a typical research objective. In social science, most studies are conducted at the dyadic level to answer questions such as: "What is the basis of friendship ties or how do firms pick alliance partners?" (Borgatti 2009)

This involves the question surrounding the formation mechanisms of social relations. Why are some people more closely connected than others, or why do they build cliques in the network or remain isolated?

In the following we will demonstrate, using some examples, the explanations researchers have provided for observed network structures. The selection presented is small and makes no claim of completeness. Its purpose is to illustrate a variety of social science problems, in which the network is the dependent variable.

Attribute-based Explanations

Social relations, in general, and friendship relations, in particular, show whether friends are more similar according to socio-demographic characteristics, social structure, or attitudes than would be expected from random associations.

For example, a comprehensive study carried out by Claude Fischer (1982) in Northern California shows that when people had freedom of choice, the networks were composed of people who were similar with regard to social background, personality, lifestyle, professional position, etc. Relatives had, for example, the same religious affiliation and belonged mostly to the same social class. Co-workers had the same professional positions. Friends had similar interests and the same education. Hence, people tend to surround themselves with people who are similar to them.

"Birds of a feather flock together" is a common saying applied to the everyday observation that the likelihood of being linked increases with the similarity of actors (McPherson, Smith-Lovin, and Cook 2001).

Lazarsfeld and Merton (1954) developed the concept of homophily for this widely empirically documented phenomenon of the similarity of interrelated actors (McPherson et al. 2001). Homophily is the tendency of individuals to associate and bond with similar others. The presence of homophily has been discovered in a vast array of network studies. In their extensive review paper, McPherson et al. (2001) cite over 100 studies that observed homophily in some form. These include age, gender, class, organizational role, and so forth.

In their original formulation of homophily Lazarsfeld and Merton (1954) distinguished between status homophily and value homophily. Status homophily means that individuals with similar social status characteristics are more likely to be related to each other than to be associated by chance. By contrast, value homophily refers to a tendency to be connected with others who think in similar ways, regardless of differences in status. The pervasive fact of homophily means that cultural, behavioral, genetic, or material information that flows through networks will tend to be localized. Homophily implies that distance in terms of social characteristics is transformed into network distance (the number of relationships, through which a piece of information must travel to connect two individuals). It also implies that any social entity embedded in a social network obeys certain fundamental dynamics of its localized social area while interacting with other social entities (McPherson et al. 2001).

Rule-based Explanations

Network study analyzes and interprets the structure of relationships between persons and other units. This leads to conclusions regarding actors' positions and options for action within social networks. But what are the rules that underlie these relationships? How are these relationship initiated and how are they maintained?

Reciprocity is a basic principle for the building of relationships (e.g., Stegbauer 2010). Reciprocity means that – with the exception of unbalanced, unequal, and hierarchical forms of relationships such as child-parent, manager-employee relationships – many relationships are generally based on a mutual recognition and support. Conceptually, reciprocity overlaps with exchange. Exchange is dominated by complementary

Box 4: Merton's Scientists

The idea of preferential attachment was first introduced by Robert K. Merton (1968). Being a sociologist, Merton was interested in understanding the internal dynamics of science as a social system. He had observed that scientists who were already famous often gained in popularity and influence in their scientific field even though other – often younger and less visible – colleagues made more significant contributions to the field. This pattern is visible when we look at the way in which credit is distributed among researchers involved in a collaborative project. Merton's observations and interviews with Nobel laureates confirm that the scientists who are already famous will be credited for an innovation irrespective of how much they actually contributed to the project. Merton calls this the Matthew effect, citing the Gospel in which St. Matthew stated: "For unto every one that hath shall be given, and he shall have abundance: but from him that hath not shall be taken away even that which he hath." (Matthew 13:12) Merton's analysis concludes that science is a reputational economy that makes it very difficult for young members of the community to gain status (Merton 1968).

needs that should be satisfied by the exchange. Reciprocity is applied more permanently and is characterized by reciprocal commitments, the same entity of exchange being involved on both sides of the equation in many cases (e.g., recognition being exchanged for recognition).

An example of reciprocal relations is scientific cooperation. While giving and receiving are temporally shifted, the relationship is based on mutual recognition. If inequality persists, the relationship is dissolved. If a reciprocity norm for the network to be analyzed is adopted, it is assumed that asymmetrical relations will be reciprocated or canceled in the long run.

Explanations Based on Network Position

Actors with many contacts and actors with few, or even no, contacts can be identified by analyzing network structures. Why do some people have many ties and others only have very few, or why are some actors connected and others not? Some approaches postulate that the decision to

Box 5: Milgram's Six Degrees of Separation

This situation is familiar to all of us: You meet a stranger (e.g., while on vacation) and figure out a friend you have in common with that stranger. "It's a small world" is a much-used saying. In his most famous experiment of the 1960s, Stanley Milgram (1967) selected 296 random individuals from two cities in the USA (Omaha, Nebraska, and Wichita, Kansas) and asked them to forward an initial letter to a target contact person located in Boston. Participants were asked to either forward the letter to the target if they actually knew the person, or to forward it to a person of their acquaintance that was the most likely to know the target contact person. Result: only 20 percent of the letters sent reached their target, yielding an average chain length of 6.5 (although this number does not take into account the remaining 80 percent of the letters).

engage in and maintain a social tie is related to position in the network. People choose others because they are already central or peripheral, well-connected or isolated, not because they are rich or poor.

One way credit is expressed in science is by citations. Merton (1968) observes that people who are already famous and much-cited can easily acquire new citations (see Box 4). The probability of being cited, a link in a scientific social network, is thus proportional to the citations received in the past. This observation fits very well with Price's observation that scientific citations follow a very unequal distribution. While few authors and papers get cited a lot, most are not cited at all (Price 1976). The unequal distribution of choices in social networks has already been noted by the founding father of network analysis: Jacob L. Moreno. Moreno found that friendship choices in school classes followed a very unequal distribution: some get named a lot and others only very selectively. He was so convinced by this pattern that he called it the "second sociometric law." (Moreno 1934; 1953) Barabási and Albert (1999) use this idea to create random networks with power-law degree distributions. They call the effect whereby the new nodes in the network are more likely to connect with well-connected nodes "preferential attachment."

Box 6: Balance Theory

Balance theory (Heider 1946) is based on the assumption that social perception follows gestalt-like structural principles and preference is given to balanced states over unbalanced states.

Heider considers dyadic or triadic configurations consisting of a perceiving person i, another person j, and an impersonal object x: The relationships between the units are either positive or negative. Each individual relationship between these units is interdependent on the other relationships. If, for example, i has a positive attitude to j, and j is attached to x, i will also tend to develop a positive attitude to x. As a result, the relationships tend to be balanced. In general, a balanced configuration exists when the attitudes to the parts of a causal unit are similar (cf. Heider 1946). In terms of network analysis, the object x is usually interpreted as a third person (cf. Newcomb 1953); therefore this constellation is a triad. Hence, if a person i is positively disposed towards person j but person x does not like person j, an imbalanced state prevails. According to Heider, an imbalanced state would lead to tensions, hence either the signs in front of the connecting ties change or the relationships are altered through actions (cf. Heider 1946). This would mean that either person x tries to like person j or that an actor in the triad would tend to dissolve the relationship. Heider's ideas were transferred to networks. The basic principle is that single objects, e.g., people, are represented as a node and edges exist between these nodes, if a certain relation (for example, acquaintanceship) exists.

Explanations Based on Patterns of Relation

Milgram (1967) analyzed the average path length of the social networks of people in the USA. This established the research connected with the term "small world" within sociology (Kochen 1989).

The small-world property of networks describes the simultaneity of densely connected groups of nodes, and short average distances in sparse networks. Watts and Strogatz (1998) exemplifies that random networks with these properties can be obtained from a generative model.

The comparison of empirical networks with idealized random networks shows that social networks often have more cohesive group structures (Heidler 2008). For example, small-world networks (Milgram 1967;

Watts and Strogatz 1998), which can be detected in various contexts, have a locally cohesive group structure with short overall distances. A cohesive group is a set of actors whose internal network density is greater than the external density (Davis 1963). Such a cohesive group structure can be derived from balance-theory considerations (see Box 6).

Two phenomena are observed in small-world networks. First, the probability is very high that two nodes that are connected to a third node will also be connected to each other. When applied to social networks, this means that a person's friends are usually well known to each other because they have met through their mutual friend.

Second, the diameter of these networks is relatively small. This means that, in each case, a message is passed from one node over an edge to all of its neighboring nodes, and rapidly reaches all nodes in the network.

The first observed phenomenon is also known as transitivity. The underlying assumption is that a transitive cognition "balance" mechanism is developed in social communities aiming to overcome dissonance and achieve consistency in cognition among actors (Heider 1946; Festinger 1957; Cartwright and Harary 1956). For example, when dissonances arise between people, they attempt to reduce them by persuading others, who will persuade more people and so on.

Combined Explanations

Nevertheless, a single approach is often insufficient to explain the observed network structure. Sophisticated models for explaining the emergence of social structure combine different approaches to attain maximum explanatory power.

Bearman et al. (2004) offer a combined explanation for the two phenomena. Homophily with respect to sexual experiences can explain the connectedness of the network. It cannot, however, account for the low level of cohesion. To explain the long chains of affection, the authors included a local pattern of partner selection in the model. The presence of excessively short cycles in sexual relationships causes conflicts. When the authors excluded cycles of length four from the partner selection process, a pattern emerged that can explain both salient network properties. (Bearman et al. 2004)

Box 7: Adolescent Sexuality

Bearman, Moody, and Stovel (2004) were interested in learning how social and sexual networks are formed among adolescents in the USA. Knowledge about the structure of sexual networks is of major importance for understanding the transmission of sexually transmitted diseases. The data they analyzed were collected among 832 students from a high school in the U.S. mid-west. The adolescents listened to the questions via earphones and entered their responses directly into a computer, thereby eliminating interviewer or parental effects on their responses. They were asked to identify their sexual and romantic partners using a unique ID.

The almost complete sexual and romantic network data was collected from the saturated field settings. During the in-home interviews, the adolescents were asked whether they were or had been involved in a "special romantic relationship" at some point in the past 18 months. The adolescents who were, or had been, involved in such relationships were asked to describe their three most recent relationships, including any current relationships, and to identify their relationship partners. They were also asked to identify up to three individuals, with whom they had had a non-romantic sexual relationship in the past 18 months. A non-romantic sexual relationship was defined as a relationship involving sexual intercourse that the respondent did not identify as special and in which the partners did not kiss, hold hands, or say that they liked each other.

Start and end dates for all romantic and non-romantic sexual partnerships were collected for the vast majority of reported partnerships. Following the collection of detailed information about partnerships, the respondents were asked whether their partners attended their school (or the middle school that fed students into the high school). If their partners attended either school, the respondents were asked to identify their partners using a unique ID.

Apart from obtaining information about social and sexual linkages, the study also recorded demographic characteristics and tastes and other attributes. An exploratory analysis of the network structure revealed two important features: Many of the students were connected through sexual relationships and the network displays very little cohesion and displays a tree-like span.

Network Structure as the Outcome of Certain Conditions

Perhaps the most fundamental proposition in social network research is that an actor's position in a network determines, in part, the opportunities and constraints that the actor encounters and, in this way, plays an important role in the network outcomes. This is the network thinking behind the popular concept of social capital, which in one formulation posits that the rate of return on an actor's investment in their human capital (i.e., their knowledge, skills, and abilities) is determined by their social capital (i.e., their network location).

The network is an opportunity structure that arises from investments in social relations. Social capital is an investment in social relations (Bourdieu 1983). Banal though it may seem, it is important to note that one cannot invest if one does not belong. In other words, the possibility of such an investment requires "admission" or eligibility. For example, it is a privilege to study at the University of the Sorbonne in France, however admission to the university is subject to certain conditions. The Sorbonne is an elite university and it is difficult for someone who is not part of the elite to study there. Hence, it may be also a privilege to invest in specific networks and create standardized structures that are located and maintained in this way, even if the "return on the investment" is unclear. Thus, it is important to know who has access to a network and who does not. In this respect the structure of a network is the result of certain conditions.

Granovetter (1985) argues that market relations are embedded in social relations. One could also argue that the opposite is the case: i.e., social relations are embedded in market relations. The social network, which must protect market transactions against opportunism or to ruinous competition, is preformed by functional interdependencies both between its members and in terms of forms of exchange.

In Summary

Dyads form the basis of network analysis. These are relations between two actors. The focus of interest in network analysis is, therefore, on social relationships and the structure and functions of interpersonal and organizational networks. Most network research starts with an exploratory phase and the description of a network. Network descriptions offer new insights to relatively unknown phenomena and populations (Lundberg), or enable the testing of different theoretical predictions about the social world (Wellman).

Box 8: Windolf's Elites

Paul Windolf (2009) provides examples of investments in social relations. From time to time, Elbert H. Gary, who was chairman of the U.S. Steel Corporation from 1901 to 1927, invited the top executives of competing steel companies to dinner. The first dinner was held in November 1907 and brought together 51 leaders of the U.S. steel industry. The Committee on Investigations of U.S. Steel Corp. asked Gary about these practices in 1911 and he stated for the record: "The question was how to get between the two extremes of securing a monopoly by driving out competition ... or how to maintain prices without making any agreement, express or implied, tacit or otherwise. And so, gentlemen, I invited a large percentage of the steel interests of the country to meet me at dinner..." (cited in Laidler 1931: 47)

Villa Herbertshof, where Herbert M. Gutmann, a member of the board of Dresdner Bank 1910–1931, resided fulfilled a similar function.

The festivities organized at this villa fulfilled "especially the function of a central meeting place of the Berlin Society and served as Gutmann's exclusive town homes on the Pariser Platz maintaining contacts with the diplomatic corps, the Berlin government bureaucracy and the nobility." (Münzel 2006: 217)

The market and the division of labor constitute a system of technical and economic interdependency. This exchange system provides the context for a social network in the market. Gary's guests included steel managers, engineers, lawyers, and bankers and it is unlikely that there were any sociologists or pastors in these networks. In terms of its members, its implications in structure, and exchange relations, the network is rooted in this system of functional interdependence.

Whether you go beyond the description of networks, depends on what should be explained by the network.

Hence the first question that must be clarified for the research design is what should be explained by the network, i.e., is the network the dependent or explanatory variable in the research design? This means that if you wish to explain how the network influences the behavior of individuals or groups, the network is an explanatory variable, and if you wish to explain the ways in which individuals are related or how certain networks or relations arise, the network is the dependent variable. Using the example of the study carried out by Bott, we tried to demonstrate the effects the network has on the division of labor in the family. In this case, the network is the explanatory variable.

The examples provided of the network as the dependent variable have shown that there are different prerequisites for the formation of social relations or networks.

For example, as illustrated by the example of homophily, networks can originate from similar actor characteristics. Reciprocity can also constitute a rule for the formation of social relationships. Such relationships are often found in scientific cooperation.

While homophily and reciprocity were selected as examples of explanations that postulate initial mechanisms of social relations, the other examples presented characteristics that are the result of the properties of the network and their own dynamics. This included the declaration of the network structure formed from the positioning of actors within the network (Merton, Moreno, Barabási & Albert) or the small world studies (Milgram, Watts & Strogatz), the explanation of which is based on the cohesive group structure in the network.

However, as should have been demonstrated by the example of Bearman et al.'s study, a single approach is often not sufficient to explain the network structure. In this study, the structure of social relations was explained in part by the similarity of the actor's characteristics and by the local selection pattern.

The example of social capital helps to clarify that existing structures can have an impact on the position an actor can assume in a network or whether the actor remains excluded from a network. In this regard, the structure of a network is the result of certain preceding conditions. To summarize, it may be noted that the explanations of the network as dependent variable can be based on attributes, the social settings, or the position of the actors, which can result, in turn, from existing structures.

Finally, it is important to note that the cause-effect connection of networks is not always easy to separate, as demonstrated by the following example.

A typical example here is the phenomenon of smoking friendship networks in school. It can frequently be observed that students who smoke are also friends with each other. The question, therefore, is whether students who are friends with each other smoke because they have adapted to their smoking friends, or whether smokers are friends because they already smoked anyway and have selected themselves as friends on the basis of this similarity? Is it a matter of influence or selection? The concept of influence argues that network structure affects the attitudes and behavior of the actors. Influence means that players, for example, adapt their attitudes to the actors with whom they are linked. The mechanism of selection observes the process conversely: attributional characteristics affect the network structure. The concept of selection argues that social linkages (existence or non-existence of a link) or positions that derive from direct and indirect linkages may be explained through attributes. This example shows that a network is actually a combination of structure and individual characteristics, i.e., that the change in the individual characteristic "smoking" is a property that arises from the network. In other words, the network effects itself. Thus, selection and influence have endogenous effects. This means that, in this case, the origin and effect of the network are mutual.

2.3 Typology of Networks

Similar to whether the network itself serves as the dependent or independent variable, the types of social networks can be differentiated on the basis of the dependencies in which the actors are considered: Is the focus of inquiry the effects of the social embeddedness of an actor in his or her environment or is the network being used to describe a social structure? This, in turn, is closely related to the research question.

The network type analysis used by Granovetter in his study is called the ego-centered network. The complete network is another type of network. This type differs from the ego-centered network in that, in this instance, the individuals define each other's environment (e.g., in a school class, or an organization). In this case we obtain information on the number of actor and all dyad relations in a particular unit. For instance, if

Box 9: Granovetter's Job Seekers

In "Getting a Job," Mark S. Granovetter (1974) was primarily interested in the influence of social capital on the job search process. He examined males from Newton, a suburb of Boston, who were in paid employment in occupations from the fields of management, the professions, and technology. In a comparison of urban directories (which also contain information about the occupation and the employer) for subsequent years, persons were identified who had changed employer or were newly registered. The 50 percent sample included 515 job-changers, of whom 300 were questioned. The questions were related to the job change, the qualities of the new job (income, job satisfaction, first allocation), and, in particular, the personal contacts who had proven helpful in bringing about the job change. Granovetter's approach was influenced by the assumption that actors are embedded in social relations and their environment. In this case, the interviewees were unrelated to each other, i.e., they were independent. This made it possible to capture and compare various actors in their embeddedness and hence establish which type of embeddedness or what kind of relations support or hinder the process of the job search.

This research gave rise to Granovetter's thesis about the strength of weak ties. His results show that job-changers who received the crucial information about their new job through a work-related contact obtained a higher income than job-changers, for whom friendship and family relationships were the crucial source of information. The main contacts for the job information are dominated by weak relationships, which correspond to occasional contacts, i.e., persons with whom the frequency of contact is very low.

you would like to examine, how students' class interactions impact their academic performance, you will examine the relationships between all students in the class.

The population that needs to be studied to find the desired answer will also often arise from the research question. Social science research makes statements about selected aspects of reality. This involves the restriction of our observations and focus on certain population groups, e.g., a neighborhood, company, city, immigrant community, etc. Therefore, we must now decide whether this size of group still allows the completion of a complete survey (involving interviews with all members of the population) or necessitates the use of sampling techniques. The mere size of the population restricts the methods that we may use to study their networks.

The unit of analysis for the network study is determined on the basis of the research questions relating to the completeness and variety of interactions.

2.3.1 Complete Networks

The concept of a complete network is not absolute and must always be viewed in relation to the unit of analysis as empirical studies are always limited and cannot capture reality in its totality. Hence, the modeling of complete networks is not carried out on the level of individual interactions but relates to social units and social aggregates, for example, companies or parties, which are interpreted as active units. On the level of individual interactions, complete networks are used for the analysis of selected interactions between all members of a unit of analysis. This modeling of social relationships is called a partial network. In practical application, however, the selection of partial complete networks is restricted to a few spatially or socially identifiable objects of investigation. Partial complete networks, especially in sociometry (see the work of Moreno 1967), form the first empirical applications in the research history of social networks form. The study of a complete network considers both the occurrence and non-occurrence of relations between all members of a population. A complete network describes the ties that all members of a population maintain with all others in the group.

The effects of the interaction on the relationships between the actors and how they are examined depend on the research question. In other words, it depends on the research question who the actors to be examined are and what kind of relationship exists between them.

There are two essential types of complete networks, one-mode networks and two-mode networks.

One-mode Networks

A one-mode network involves the measurements of just a single set of actors. The actors can be people, subgroups, organizations, or collectives and aggregates, such as communities and nation-states. The relations on the level of pairs of actors in a one-mode network can be viewed as representing specific substantive connections. These connections can be of many types. The type of relation to be captured depends on the research question.

Knoke and Kuklinski (1982: 16) provide classifications for the contents of relations:

- Transaction relations, in which limited resources are transferred, e.g., purchases, gifts.
- Communication relations, in which actors act as channels through which messages may be transmitted form one actor to another in a system.
- Instrumental relations, in which actors contact each another in an effort to secure services or information, etc.
- Sentiment relations, in which individuals express their feelings of affection, admiration, deference, etc.
- Power relationships, which indicate the rights and obligations of actors to issue and obey commands.
- Kinship relations, which indicate relationships between family members.

One or more of these relationship types may be measured for a single set of actors. In addition to relational information, the social network data set can contain actor attribute variables, such age, gender, race, socioeconomic status, place of residence, etc. "For corporate actors, one can measure their profitability, revenues, geographical location, purpose of business and so on" (Wasserman and Faust 1994: 39).

Two-mode Networks

A two-mode network consists of two sets of distinct units (e.g., people and events), and the relations that are measured between the two sets, e.g., participation of people in social events.

An example of a two-mode network can be found in the work of the Chicago sociologists Davis, Gardner, and Gardner (1941), who traced the social life in a city ("Old City") in the southern United States through a community study carried out over a period of two years in the 1940s using the instrument of participant observation.

Their work provides, *inter alia*, information about the participation of 18 upper-class women in 14 important events in the city. The details of these actor-event linkages are based on observations, interviews, and newspaper reports.

In this example, the data are not restricted to a set of actors and their relationships with each other, but relate elements from two sets to each other, i.e., the set of the actors (women) and the set of the events. The social relationship relates to the participation of actors in the events (i.e., present at the event or not).

Events, at which these women were present at the same time, create social similarities between them. The patterns of participation provide information on the status of the actors in the community. With the addition of a second mode, the relationship of interest can be better circumscribed and patterns of social order may be deduced from it (Schweizer 1996).

Various types of two-mode networks are formed by the following combinations:

- Membership of institutions: people, institutions are members, e.g., directors and officers on the boards of corporations.
- Voting on political proposals: politicians, the casting of votes on proposals.
- "Buying articles in a shop" whereby the first set consists of consumers and the second of articles; the connection indicates which article was bought by a consumer.
- Readers and magazines.
- Citation network, in which the first set consists of authors, the second set consists of articles/papers and the connection is a relation whereby an author cites a paper.

Hence, the different type of actors, the types of relations, and the types of actor attributes are the same for one-mode networks. In a two-mode network with two sets of actors, at least one relation is measured between actors in the two sets. In a more extensive two-mode network data set, relations can also be defined for actors within a set. At least one relation must be defined between the two sets of actors.

Most social network analysis is concerned with the one-mode case, as in the analysis of friendship ties among a set of school children or advice-giving relations within an organization. The two-mode case arises when researchers collect relations between classes of actors, such as persons and organizations, or persons and events. For example, a researcher might collect data on which students at a university belong to which campus organizations, or which employees in an organization participate in which electronic discussion forums. These kinds of data are often referred to as affiliations. Co-memberships in organizations or participation in events are typically thought of as providing opportunities for social relationships among individuals (and also as the consequences of pre-existing relationships). At the same time, ties between organizations through their members are thought to be conduits, through which organizations influence each other (see Borgatti 2009).

2.3.2   Ego-centered Networks

The ego-centered network approach originates in anthropology and its roots go back to the work of Alfred R. Radcliffe-Brown (1940; 1957), among others. In this case, social relations based on a person are considered (Barnes 1972). This type of network is used when the actors are regarded as independent of each other and their embeddedness is the subject of research.

Ego networks are typically conducted when the identities of the egos are known, but not their alteri. These studies rely on the egos to provide information about the identities of their alteri and there is no expectation that the various egos or sets of alteri will be tied to each other. Ego networks are designed to capture individual social environments and thereby lift the numerical restriction on the selection of fewer units of examination. They are suitable for use in mass representative surveys and allow for inferential analysis. They also enable the comparison of the structure of interpersonal environments for individual characteristics, for variables of the social context and the geographical environment.

Ego-centered social network analysis is concerned with making generalizations about the features of personal networks that explain things like longevity, consumer and voting behavior, coping with difficult life situations, economic success or failure, etc. With its focus on individuals, the

Box 10: Personal Networks of Migrants

In a study of the personal networks of migrants (Molina, Lerner, and Mestres 2008; Brandes, Lerner, Lubbers, McCarty, and Molina 2008), more than 500 immigrants to Spain and the USA were surveyed. Each of the personal network describes the social environment of an immigrant originating from a South-American, Central-American, African or Eastern-European country. Each respondent was asked to provide four types of information. There were questions about the respondent himself/herself, including age, skin color, years of residence, questions from traditional acculturation scales, and health-related questions. Other question collected a list of 45 persons (referred to as alters) personally known to the respondent and information about each of the alteri, including country of origin, country of residence, skin color, and type of relation to ego. And, last but not least, there was a question about each of the 990 undirected pairs of alters: "What is the likelihood that Alter 1 and Alter 2 have a relationship independent of you?" which the respondent (ego) answered by choosing between the possible replies "very likely," "maybe," or "unlikely." The relations were binarized with "very likely" as the threshold.

ego network approach has proven more germane to studies of community than the complete network approach. It is also possible to treat organizations, classrooms, communities, or even nations as the ego in an ego network study. Such an ego network consists of the individual ego-alter dyads and additional information on the contact links and understanding of the social network among individuals.

Ego networks can also be distinguished in two ways for describing the embeddedness of actors in social relations. First, there are ego-centered networks that describe the direct relation of an ego to its alteri. In addition, there are personal networks which, in addition to the direct relation between ego and alter, also cover the structure of the environment through the relations between the alteri.

Individual determinants of egocentric networks, for example the levels of heterogeneity and homogeneity and specific communication roles such as opinion leaders and the recipients of the communication, can be extrapolated from the answers provided by the ego-alter dyads. Specifications of

network type	unit of analysis	level of analysis
complete	*one-mode:* includes the relationships between actors of the same type	all dyads
	two-mode: includes the relationships that exist between two sets of units (people or events)	all dyads in each single dataset and dyads, in which the first actor and the second actor in the dyad are from different set
ego-centered	*ego network:* focuses on an actor and his relation with the environment	dyads of a person (ego-alter dyads) and network structure of these dyads
	personal network: focuses on an actor and his relation to the environment and the structure of the environment	dyads of a person (ego-alter dyads), the network structure of these dyads and alter-alter dyads.

Figure 4: Typology of social networks.

alter-alter relations are needed if, for example, the network closure needs to be determined, thus for central descriptive parameters of the network structure. Closure, here refers to the relation of the actual alteri contacts with the potentially possible alteri contacts. In network analysis, closure is used to describe a generalized harmony among the various alteri. The microstructure of the ego-centered network, which can be used for typical network analyses about triads, cliques, and bridge features as well as for the balance theory of social relations, can be gleaned from this analysis (see Chapter 4).

Figure 4 summarizes the different types of networks, the unit of analysis, and the levels of analysis.

2.4 Longitudinal Network Studies

The research designs introduced so far limit descriptions and explanations to a single point in time. However, networks are dynamic and changing. The most common approaches for studying the dynamics of social networks are panel surveys. To understand how social structures develop or change over time, the same data collection technique is repeated at different points in time, yielding two or more snapshots of the social setting.

One of the first studies of this kind was Newcomb's work on the evolution of friendship in a U.S. college fraternity (see Box 13). He was interested in testing how social relationships and attitudes towards abstract objects co-exist and co-emerge.

Newcomb distinguishes between the relationship between two actors, i and j, and an attitude x. He assumes that social relationships are more likely to emerge between i and j if i thinks that j has the same attitude towards x that he has (Newcomb 1961: 9). The idea is based on Heider's balance theory and Newcomb carried out the first longitudinal study to test it.

Hence, he invited 17 formerly unacquainted male students to stay free of charge at a U.S. college fraternity house. In return, they had to participate in an interview every week, in which they ranked all 16 other members of the group according to their *favorableness*. The data resulted in 15 waves of observations about the social structure of 17 students, which Newcomb mostly analyzed using standard statistical techniques (Newcomb 1961). The results show that likes choose likes and, more particularly, that people with similar attitudes when they arrived at the fraternity tended to become friends later. While the attitudes did not change much over the time span observed, the social structure did to some degree. A recent re-analysis of the data using network techniques showed that many of the structural properties of the network developed very fast. As early as week 0 and by week 4 at the latest, most of the subgroups and individual positions that characterized the network at the end of the study period had emerged. Relatively few changes occurred over the course of the weeks after the initial formation (Trappmann, Hummell, and Sodeur 2005).

New analytical techniques enable the use of data collected at two or more points in time to explain the changes between two points in time. These rules can be related to characteristics of ego and alter, for example age and gender. They may also relate to their position in the network or

Box 11: Powell's Biotech Industry

One example is the data collected by Walter W. Powell, White, Koput, and Koput (2005) on the evolution of cooperation in biotech firms in the USA. The data are drawn from an industry directorate, BioScan. The data cover a number of distinct relationships that are reported every year. Unlike the data discussed so far, the data from the directorates provide the exact dates when a relationship was formed and when it dissolved. This allowed Powell and his collaborators to study the process of the formation of an industry field over a period of 12 years. Like other studies, most of the analysis separates the data into different time slices to test four different hypotheses about that govern the formation. The analysis reveals that the most fundamental attachment rule is towards multiconnectivity and diversity, that is to link with varied partners who are broadly linked. This logic is robust and leads to the creation of cohesive and well-connected networks over the entire period of time considered (Powell et al. 2005: 1189).

their former interactions. Those models have developed into very powerful tools for understanding how contexts and structures interact and which micro-rules lead to which macro-level structural results (Snijders, van de Bunt, and Steglich 2010; Steglich and Knecht 2010).

If events are time-structured, more strategies for analyzing the dynamics of social networks become available. This is the case if social relationships are reconstructed from archives, in which they are identified with an event: an email written at a certain point in time, a god-parenthood relationship initiated through a baptism on a certain date, or a vote from a politician on some parliamentary issue are relationships that can be traced to an exact date (Schnegg 2007). Unfortunately, very few techniques exist for analyzing these data as continuous information. Researchers very often group these events in time slices and analyze their change in ways comparable to the strategies outlined above.

2.5 Summary

If you are planning research, in which social relations appear to be relevant, you must first answer the question concerning the purpose served by the network analysis. If you would like to make new phenomena visible, the description of network connections is sufficient in many cases. If a network is used to explain social phenomena, you must decide whether the network is the dependent or independent variable (see Section 2.2).

After this question has been clarified, you must then consider which data are necessary to answer the research question. Before collecting any data, you must choose the relevant unit of analysis, the relevant relationship (form and content), and the level of data analysis.

Determining the Level of Analysis

The level of aggregation (definition of actors) that is relevant for the study depends on the research question.

Depending on the research question, a network researcher must decide on the most relevant type of social organizations and the level of aggregation within that social form comprised by the network nodes. This may be individuals, groups (formal or informal), complex formal organizations, communities, classes, and strata or nation-states. The network researcher must also decide how many modes the network has, i.e., one or two (see Figure 4).

Determining a Type of Network

The choice of the relevant level of aggregation is also closely linked to the choice of network type. The selection between an ego network or a complete network approach depends on two factors: (i) the research question; and (ii) the size and the availability of the researched population. The first question relates to the crucial difference as to whether you wish to explain the embeddedness of actors and the way that shapes their behavior or whether you are shining the spotlight of the analysis on the internal structure of the group. However, if you wish to focus on the group as a whole, you may find that the group is too big or access is too difficult to enable you to study all of the links between all members.

We differentiate between two types of networks, i.e., personal networks and complete networks. In both cases the researcher selects who or what is to be studied and the ties to be considered. Let us take as an example school children and their friendship relationships. In the case of complete networks, we determine for all actors whether or not relationships with all other members of the group exist. This necessitates the definition of the boundaries of the group. In the case of school children, this could be a single class, a grade, the school, or even a larger frame such as all school children in a region or a country. With ego networks, in contrast, you determine for all actors in the sample, with whom they have ties of the selected kind. Hence, through the study of ego networks we can (and often will) obtain information about actors outside of the initial sample. This is not the case with complete networks where we only learn about ties among those interviewed.

More substantially, complete network and ego network analyses are two research designs that correspond to two fundamentally different research tasks:

1. For complete networks: Which relationships does an actor in a group maintain (or not) with each of the other members of the group?
2. For ego networks: Which relationships of a given kind does each member of a group maintain with other actors, irrespective of whether they are part of the group?

Ego networks may overlap (an ego is an alter in another network). If this is the case, we can combine them and analyze them, in part, as a complete network. This may arise if all members of a group are interviewed and ties have been selected that are largely maintained among members of that same group.

While many empirical network studies fall into one of the two categories – ego or complete networks – in recent years, a considerable number of "hybrids" falling between these two extremes have emerged. These aim to overcome the specific limitations inherent in the two approaches by adding either "openness" to complete networks or "structure" to personal ones.

Determining a Relation of Interest

The relations that are relevant to the analysis must be defined for all network analyses. The relations between actors have both content and form. Content refers to the substantive type of relation represented by the connection (e.g., supporting, supervising). An inventory of content types may be found in Section 2.3.1 (one-mode networks) and in Knoke and

Kuklinski (1982). The form of relations refers to properties of connection between pairs of actor (dyads) that exist independently of specific contents. For example, the intensity or strength of the relation between two actors or the level of joint involvement in the same activities (see Knoke and Kuklinski 1982).

This chapter has introduced you to different research designs. We have seen that "one size does not fit all" and the development of a research design involves many decisions. The following questions bundle some of the thoughts presented and provide guidance in the choice and development of a research strategy:

1. What do you want to achieve?
   Networks sometimes become an independent or a dependent variable and you wish to explain what causes their specific structure and what they cause. Which applies in your case?
2. How big is the population you wish to study?
   If the population is larger than approximately 200 individuals, complete networks are very difficult to reconstruct unless the social relationships you wish to study are archived.
3. Does your research question focus on the internal structure of a population or the embeddedness of actors?
   If the former is the case, you must include a component that can capture that dimension (complete network, ego network). If the latter is the case, you must include a personal network component, possibly in combination with a complete network approach (if the population is small and cohesive enough).
4. Do you need to understand change over time?
   In this case, you must repeat the data collection process using any of the study designs.

2.6 Exercises

1. Suppose you would like to investigate whether personality traits influence friendship relations by studying a group of university students.

Design a study by

- formulating a hypothesis based on homophily,

- listing (network and non-network) variables that you would like to include,

- explaining the role of each variable, and

- describing (in general terms) how they relate to your hypothesis.

Are you looking for status or value homophily?

2. Repeat the first exercise with the following modifications:

- Redesign the study to investigate whether cooperative behavior is related to academic achievement.

- Redesign the study to investigate whether cooperation is affected by students getting to know each other better.

Discuss the influence of these modifications on your design and explicate the causality assumptions in your design.

3. How do designs for studies involving ego networks differ from non-network studies involving population samples?

4. Explain the differences between ego-centered and complete networks. What determines which type of network is sought in a study? Give examples.

5. Give examples for relationships between actors that can be derived from two-mode networks. Do they differ from other relations that define one-mode networks?

3 Data

In this chapter you will learn what is special about network data and its collection. You will be able to differentiate between data about actors and data about relations between them, and thus be able to identify the kind of data required for an empirical study using any of the network types introduced in the previous chapter. We will also discuss straightforward ways of organizing various types of data.

The distinctive characteristic of network studies is their relational perspective. This perspective is reflected most clearly in the type of data used. Attributes are collected and analyzed not only for actors, such as persons or organizations, but also, and even more importantly, for the relations between them. A dyadic attribute is an attribute associated with pairs of actors, not just individual actors, and because each actor appears in several of these pairs, there are inherent and inevitable dependencies. Unlike in population studies, in which dependencies among actors are often considered a nuisance, they are the primary focus of interest in network studies.

In the simplest case, dyadic data only differentiate between the existence or non-existence of a relationship. In more complex scenarios, however, ties can be comprised of multiple relationships, each of which may require more detailed representation than a binary variable. For instance, if you are studying contact networks, you would be expecting relevant variation across media (face-to-face, phone calls, emails, etc.) and intensities of communication. It would be careless, therefore, to record only the pair of actors that communicates sufficiently to match some definition of "being in contact."

In the following section we will differentiate between the various types of network data and then focus on their collection. We will also discuss quality issues and some ethical considerations for studies involving humans at the end of this chapter.

3.1   Kinds of Data

Network studies are grounded in theories about the antecedents and consequences of social relations between actors. Hence, they make use of data that differ from those in population studies. In this section, we will clarify what exactly this difference entails. In fact, the type of data studied represents the most precise distinction between population studies and network studies.

3.1.1   Units and Levels

Data generally refers to the *values* of a collection of *variables*. In an empirical study, variables are associated with the *entities* of interest, and usually describe their properties. Depending on the possible expressions of a property, variables have values in different *ranges*.

For example, it is convenient to describe the height of a person in a *numerical range* such as decimal numbers because height is a measurable quantity. In contrast, hair color appears to be more appropriately described by a category label, and is thus a *nominal variable*. The range of labels is either standardized or crafted for the study. Numerical variables are often referred to as *quantitative* while nominal variables are called *qualitative*, however this distinction is neither useful nor unanimous. For instance, if height is not expressed in centimeters but by classification into short, medium, and tall, we obtain an *ordinal* variable. Ordinal variables can be meaningfully compared by rank but not by differences or ratios. While mathematically inclined analysts would probably classify ordinal variables as qualitative because they do not represent quantities in a formal sense, more qualitatively-oriented researchers might still refer to them as them quantitative because they admit formal treatment. We shall not take sides in this debate.

A collection of variables representing the same kind of property for a group of entities is often called an *attribute* or a *feature* of that group.

The entities, for which we collect (or someone else has collected) data are called the *units of observation*. The reason for this is that, even when such entities, like companies, are aggregates, they are the finest level of detail considered during data collection. Otherwise, it would also be necessary to obtain data on the constituents, which would make the constituents the units of observation.

The *level of analysis* is the level, for which we would like to obtain results. Like the unit of observation, the *unit of analysis* is defined by the entities that are characterized by the data used in an analysis.

The units of observation and analysis need not be the same, however. Assume for example, we are conducting an ego-centered network study and collect data about the ties between egos and their alteri. Then the variables representing this data are indexed with ego-alter dyads, which are, therefore, the unit of observation. If we then compare egos by the size of their networks, we are actually comparing numbers associated to the egos. Hence, the size attribute is indexed by the egos which are, therefore, the unit of analysis.

Network studies differ from more common population studies, most notably by their units of observation. In addition to actor attributes, i.e., variables indexed by actors, they crucially involve tie attributes. While actor attributes are the same type of data as those used in population studies, the units of observation for relational attributes are overlapping dyads. Dyads are composite entities, however the main differences arise because actors participate in multiple dyads.

The reasons why the process of deciding on the units may not be as obvious as it seems are outlined briefly below. For a more detailed treatment of the choice of representation, see Butts (2009).

Actors

Actors are an elementary unit of observation because, in most cases, you will be interested in having at least some attribute information about them, even if the core interest is the relations between them.

However, clarifying the precise entities that form the set of actors may be less obvious than it seems. As in any socio-empirical study, actors can be *individual* (or *personal*), such as humans or animals, or they can be *aggregate* (or *corporate*), such as couples, flocks, or organizations. The decision for a particular unit of observation is a theoretical one because it should match the acting units in the social system being studied. In a study involving the analysis of economic exchange processes among pastoral nomads, it may be appropriate to conceptualize households as the interacting units. In a study of social support among villagers in an industrialized society, on the other hand, households are probably too coarse a granularity. The important distinction need not be between individual and aggregate actors but could be between different levels of aggregation. This is illustrated by the choice between business units or entire companies as actors.

In addition, the theoretically informed selection of aggregation level may be complicated by pragmatic considerations such as cost or access. For example, it may be desirable for a particular research question to survey the male and female members of households separately. However, due to societal and religious factors, this may be virtually impossible on a practical level. In such cases it may be necessary to compromise on the definition of actors, and to make up for it by modifying the kind of data analyzed and the means used to collect it.

Ties

The defining characteristic of a network study is the focus on one or more relations between actors. Since the terms relation, relationship, tie, and dyad are often used with shifting or overlapping meanings, let us settle on one definition first.

We say that a pair of actors forms a *dyad*. A dyad, like an actor, is an entity, a unit of observation, defined so that we can associate variables with it. Hence, dyads serve as indices of variables but have no values themselves.

Interestingly, this is already sufficient terminology to delineate the scope of network studies: they differ from other empirical studies in that: (i) Essential units of observation are dyads; and (ii) some dyads overlap by design.

A *relationship* is a variable associated with a dyad. Such dyadic variables have three aspects: a *content*, a *direction*, and a *value*. By way of a concrete example, let us assume that we are interested in cell phone communication among a group of school children. Each pair of distinct pupils i and j forms a dyad, and we associate with each dyad the variables x_{ij} and x_{ji}, representing the number of times that i called j and j called i over a certain period of time. The variable x_{ij} represents a calling relationship (content) from i to j (direction) and has a numerical value.

The totality of all pairwise relationships that represent the same type of content makes up a *relation*. In the aforementioned example, the set of phone-call relationships defines a valued relation. A Boolean relation consists of relationships that are either present or absent but know no other values. We say that i and j *"are in* (a certain) *relation,"* if the corresponding relationship is present or has a non-zero value. If, in the above example, we are only interested in who talked to whom on the phone, irrespective of who called whom, we are studying a relation that is *symmetric* by design, i.e. $x_{ij} = x_{ji}$, and therefore also referred to as *undirected*. Note that these are features of relations and not individual relationships.

A *tie*, on the other hand, is the union of all present or non-zero relationships of a particular ordered pair i and j. Hence, a tie summarizes all relationships of a dyad in one direction. Consequently, the concept of "being tied" coincides with the concept of "being related" in the case of a single relation. In the case of several relations, a tie may consist of several relationships and is then referred to as *multiplex*. Multiplex ties can be difficult to compare if they are composed of different relationships.

Based on this terminology, the statement that a network consists of actors and the ties between them has a reasonably precise meaning.

The units of observation are dyads not ties. Ties are data on dyads. Since dyads are pairs of actors, the difficulty does not lie in finding the right level of aggregation because this is already determined by the choice of actors. Instead, it lies in the selection of dyads (all pairs? which pairs?) and, most importantly, in the definition of what constitutes a relationship.

Borgatti et al. (2009) provide a classification of example relations studied in the social sciences. We reproduce this classification in Figure 5. The collection of dyadic data shares most of its challenges with the collection of data on actors alone or any attribute data, for that matter. It should be noted, however, that some aspects are more likely to be relevant for relations. Let us discuss two such examples.

First, consider the directionality of relations. For example, we may be interested in the provision of social support among individual actors. When we conceptualize this from either the angle of giving or receiving support, we must be aware that the two relations we end up with need not be the reverse of each other. An example involving directed vs. undirected relations is friendship. While we may conceive friendship as symmetric, its expression or interpretation by interviewees may be asymmetric.

Second, some relations conceived as pair-wise are best observed indirectly via proxy data. A particular case of such indirect relations is encountered when contacts or interactions are facilitated by social settings

Similarities			Flows
Location	*Membership*	*Attribute*	
Same	Same	Same	Information
spatial	clubs	gender	Beliefs
and			Personnel
temporal	Same	Same	Resources
space	events	attitude	

Social Relations				Interactions
Kinship	*Other role*	*Affective*	*Cognitive*	
Mother of	Friend of	Likes	Knows	Sex with
	Boss of			Talked to
Sibling of	Student of	Hates	Knows about	Advice to
	Competitor of			Helped
	Student of		Sees as happy	Harmed

Figure 5: Typology of exemplary relations (Borgatti et al. 2009)

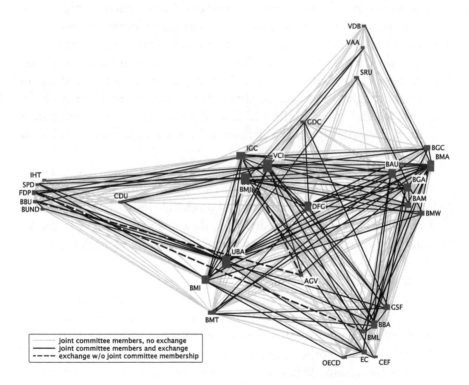

Figure 6: Joint committee membership as an infrastructure for information exchange among actors involved in a procedure for the regulation of chemicals. Redrawn from Brandes and Schneider (2009).

Box 12: Schweizer's Javanese Village

In his study of the social structure of a Javanese village, Thomas Schweizer (1996) made use of indirect relationships. So-called slametan rituals are regularly staged in the village to mark certain events in the life cycle and special occasions (e.g., harvest). Up to 200 people participate in these rituals which are organized by households. Over the course of two months, which were characterized by a particularly large number of activities (July and August 1979), Schweizer recorded who had taken part in which rituals through observation and subsequent surveys of the individual households. From these "attendance lists" he was able to reconstruct the relationships between the 98 households examined. These relationships provided information regarding who participated in a ritual, and with whom and how often they participated. He analyzed this network for the purpose of testing hypotheses on social stratification, the importance of kinship and relationships with neighbors, and the formation of social cohesion in village communities.

such as organizations or events. Figure 6 shows an example, in which this is actually a theoretical argument, and an example from an ethnographic study is provided in Box 12.

3.1.2 Organization

As we have just outlined, networks are represented by

- *actor attributes*, consisting of variables indexed by actors, and
- *tie attributes*, consisting of variables indexed by dyads.

Depending on the type of network, there will be differences in the composition of the sets of actors and dyads that index your variables, however before we describe these in more detail in the next section, let us first take a look at how attributes can be organized in data files.

While many software tools for network data analysis use their own formats for storing data in files, it is usually not necessary to read, let alone write them. The single most important format, and the only concept you really need to understand, is the data table. There are variations in the ways, in which data are arranged in tables, and we will discuss these

id	name	wealth	priors	ties
1	Acciaiuoli	10	53	2
2	Albizzi	36	65	3
3	Barbadori	55	?	14
4	Bischeri	44	12	9
5	Castellani	20	22	18
6	Ginori	32	?	9
7	Guadagni	8	21	14
8	Lamberteschi	42	0	14
9	Medici	103	53	54
10	Pazzi	48	0	7
11	Peruzzi	49	42	32
12	Pucci	3	0	1
13	Ridolfi	27	38	4
14	Salviati	10	35	5
15	Strozzi	146	74	29
16	Tornabuoni	48	?	7

Figure 7: Actor attributes represented in an actor-by-attribute table. Data provided by John Padgett for Breiger and Pattison (1986).

variations now, however, you can always think of your data as being represented in a spreadsheet.

Actor Attributes

Actor attributes are no different from attributes in other empirical studies. Each attribute is a collection of variables, one per actor, with values in a common range representing the same type of information. The conventional organization of actor attributes is a table with one row per actor and one column per attribute.

In the example given in Figure 7, actors are identified by a special attribute, ID, that has no other purpose than to disambiguate them. While it may generally be possible to identify actors via their names or some other label, this may quickly become inconvenient or even change over the course of your research. It is thus advisable to create an extra identification. As a general rule, every entity that serves as an index for variables should have a unique identifier associate with it.

Each row in Figure 7 represents a noble family in Renaissance Florence and thus an aggregate actor composed of many individuals over time. Each column represents an attribute and each cell contains the value of one variable. For instance, attribute wealth consists of the variables $\text{wealth}_1, \text{wealth}_2, \ldots, \text{wealth}_{16}$ which have values $10, 36, \ldots, 3$.

If you find yourself asking what these values represent, you have just experienced the need for a *codebook*, in which everything that it is necessary to know about what this data represents is documented. In the case of the attribute wealth, we would learn that the number represents the total wealth of a family rounded to thousands of lira in the year 1427, and that the numbers have been extracted from that year's original tax reports. The codebook would also explain that the question marks represent missing values for priors, the number of seats in the municipal council that a family occupied during the years 1282–1344. Moreover, it would point to the fact that the Pazzi have zero priors because of another role that rendered them ineligible.

The last column is interesting because it contains an index that is not directly observed but derived from tie attributes (in this case counting the number of marital and business relations, in which a family is involved). Many of the analytic techniques discussed in Chapter 4 yield such indices.

In general, all actor attributes can be stored in one table and, therefore, in one file. If actors are partitioned into groups, for which different attributes are available, however, it may be better to create one table per group of actors rather than leaving the cells that correspond to unavailable attributes empty. This is particularly common for ego-centered networks and other two-mode data, and corresponds to horizontal cuts through the table.

Vertical cuts may also be useful, for instance when the number of attributes is excessive, or different researchers work on the same data but not all of them may access all attributes. In this case, some columns may be repeated and the id-column must be repeated to avoid reliance on the order of the rows.

Tie Attributes

The focus on relational data implies that some of our attribute data is associated with composite entities, namely dyads. The index of a relational variable is thus two-dimensional, which leaves us with several alternatives as to how to organize them. In all but exceptional circumstances one of the following three alternatives will be suitable.

marital	1	2	3	4	5	6	7	8	9	10	11	12	13	14	15	16
1	0	0	0	0	0	0	0	0	1	0	0	0	0	0	0	0
2	0	0	0	0	0	1	1	0	1	0	0	0	0	0	0	0
3	0	0	0	0	1	0	0	0	1	0	0	0	0	0	0	0
4	0	0	0	0	0	0	1	0	0	0	1	0	0	0	1	0
5	0	0	1	0	0	0	0	0	0	0	1	0	0	0	1	0
6	0	1	0	0	0	0	0	0	0	0	0	0	0	0	0	0
7	0	1	0	1	0	0	0	1	0	0	0	0	0	0	0	1
8	0	0	0	0	0	0	1	0	0	0	0	0	0	0	0	0
9	1	1	1	0	0	0	0	0	0	0	0	0	1	1	0	1
10	0	0	0	0	0	0	0	0	0	0	0	0	0	1	0	0
11	0	0	0	1	1	0	0	0	0	0	0	0	0	0	1	0
12	0	0	0	0	0	0	0	0	0	0	0	0	0	0	0	0
13	0	0	0	0	0	0	0	0	1	0	0	0	0	0	1	1
14	0	0	0	0	0	0	0	0	1	1	0	0	0	0	0	0
15	0	0	0	1	1	0	0	0	0	0	1	0	1	0	0	0
16	0	0	0	0	0	0	1	0	1	0	0	0	1	0	0	0

Figure 8: Marriage relation represented in an actor-by-actor table.

participation	E1	E2	E3	E4	E5	E6	E7	E8	E9	...
A1	0	0	0	0	0	0	0	0	0	
A2	0	0	0	0	1	0	0	0	0	
A3	0	0	0	0	1	0	0	0	1	
A4	0	0	0	0	0	0	0	0	0	
A5	0	1	0	0	0	0	0	0	0	
A6	0	1	0	0	0	0	0	0	0	
A7	1	1	0	0	0	0	0	0	0	
⋮										

Figure 9: Participation relation represented in an actor-by-event table.

The first mode of organization is in actor-by-actor tables as illustrated by Figure 8. This actor-by-actor table represents a single relation, marital, among families. Rows and columns are indexed by the id-values defined for each family. A relationship between the family in row i and column j exists and is coded as $\text{marital}_{ij} = 1$, if there is at least one marriage of members from the two families. Note that this is a nominal attribute, even though it is represented by numbers. Moreover, the corresponding relation is symmetric by design. It is usually more convenient, however, to represent each pair of relationships $\text{marital}_{ij} = \text{marital}_{ji}$ explicitly.

If the actors are partitioned into two groups, such that a relationship can only exist between actors belonging to different groups (as in two-

id	id	marital	business
1	9	1	0
2	6	1	0
2	7	1	0
2	9	1	0
3	5	1	1
3	6	0	1
3	9	1	1
3	11	0	1
4	7	1	1
4	8	0	1
4	11	1	1
4	13	1	0
5	8	0	1
5	11	1	1
5	15	1	0
6	9	0	1
⋮	⋮	⋮	⋮

id	(id,marital,business)											
1	9	1	0									
2	6	1	0	7	1	0	9	1	0			
3	5	1	1	6	0	1	9	1	1	11	0	1
4	7	1	1	8	0	1	11	1	1	13	1	0
5	8	0	1	11	1	1	15	1	0			
6	9	0	1									
⋮	⋮											

(a) tie-by-attribute table
(generalized edge list)

(b) actor-ties list (generalized adjacency list)

Figure 10: Compact formats for tie attributes.

mode networks), the representation in Figure 9 is more efficient. Two-mode matrices are called *incidence matrices* when columns are interpreted as edges in a (hyper)graph representation (see Chapter 4).

The convenient actor-by-actor table form of organization has at least two shortcomings. Since table cells are usually restricted to simple numerical or textual data types, one table is required for each relation. In addition, if the number of ties is low compared to the number of dyads, matrices waste a lot of storage space.

Two alternative forms of organization that do not suffer from these shortcomings are illustrated in Tables 10(a) and 10(b).

The tie-by-attribute table is organized in exactly the same way as the actor-by-attribute table, namely by assigning one row to each tie and one column to each attribute. Since ties are identified by an ordered pair of actors, however, two columns with id-values are required. If all relations are symmetric, each dyad is listed only once. Pairs of actors, for which no relationship exists are always omitted so that much space is saved. On the other hand, it is more difficult to look up a value because the rows have to be scanned until the right index pair is found. If a sought tie does not exist, we will not find this out until we have inspected all of the ties that do exist. In the actor-by-actor table, we know exactly which cell, in which to look. This format is also called a (generalized) *edge list* because the first two columns form the list of edges in a graph representation (see Chapter 4).

The actor-ties list contains one entry for each actor. Each entry has an associated list that consists of all ties, in which the actor is involved in and all values associated with these ties. This representation is called a (generalized) *adjacency list* because each row lists the adjacencies of an actor in a graph representation (see Chapter 4). The list format summarizes all rows of the tie-by-attribute table pertaining to the same actor. It is the standard graph data structure used in software tools because it also only represents existing ties and provides more efficient access to them. If ties are symmetric and only one direction is listed, the lists of both actors must be scanned to find the attributes of a tie, or to be sure that the tie does not exist.

Since software for network analysis will be able to convert between these formats, you should select a format that is most convenient for your particular situation. When data is typed in by hand, for example, actor-by-actor tables are the most convenient format if there are only a few relations between a small number of actors. If there are too many actors to fit the entire actor-by-actor table on the screen, tie-by-attribute tables are preferable. In some cases, in which relations are few and binary and particularly when data was collected without asking the subjects about their ties, it may even be easier to list the actors' ties.

3.1.3   Which Data for Which Type of Network?

The main types of social networks have been distinguished in Chapter 2 based on the type of research question to be addressed. For these we can now state more precisely which kind of data you can expect to be dealing with in your study. Figure 11 provides an overview.

Complete Networks

Complete networks are studied when the research interest is focused on dependencies manifest in direct and indirect relations among a fixed set of actors and, possibly also, their attributes.

network/attributes	actors	ties
complete	all actors	all dyads
cognitive social structures	all actors	all dyads multiple times
two-mode	all actors in both modes	two-mode dyads only
ego	egos and alteri	ego-alter dyads
personal	egos and alteri	ego-alter and alter-alter dyads

Figure 11: Commonly used network data.

In principle, therefore, the dyads of interest are all pairs of actors. A common exception are dyads involving the same actor at both ends of a tie because this may be impossible in relations such as "child-of."

Cognitive Social Structures

Cognitive social structures are a generalization of complete networks and a special case of triadic data. Since every actor provides data for every dyad in the network, the variables are actually indexed by three actors: the one from which the value is solicited and the two forming the dyad.

Since each actor essentially provides a complete network and analyses often create aggregate dyadic data from the dyadic data provided by each actor, the usual format is as a collection of complete networks.

Similar statements apply to longitudinal networks that are available as panel data created, for example, in several rounds of data collection. Discrete observation times assume the role of actors providing their perception of a network.

Two-mode Networks

In two-mode networks, there are two kinds of actors and the relation studied is such that actors of the same kind cannot be related.

The two kinds of actors may require different attributes, hence, two actor-by-attribute tables are needed with different columns.

Note that indirect relations such as joint participation in events in the above example from Schweizer (1996) are derived from a two-mode affiliation relation. A *one-mode projection* is one of the two possible single-mode networks obtained by summarizing for a dyad of actors of the same mode their common affiliations with actors of the other mode. In the case of families participating in rituals, this is the number of jointly attended rituals or the number of families attending both rituals respectively. While there are more complicated types of summarization, one-mode projections typically correspond to multiplications of an actor-by-actor table with its transpose, or vice versa for the other mode. It is convenient, therefore, to organize a two-mode network into an actor-by-actor table with different sets of row and column actors, although software tools will also be able to work with the more compact representations.

In any event, even if your analysis is based on its one-mode projection, you should keep the original two-mode data. While you can also obtain one-mode projections, reversing the operation is not generally feasible.

Ego Networks

The purpose of an ego network study is to compare members of a population (the egos) who are characterized in part by their social environment. The attributes of interest are, therefore, both individual and relational.

The individual ego actor attributes are represented in an actor-by-attribute table as usual. Attributes of alteri, however, are typically not stored in such a table because they are not of interest independently of the respective ego. Since there is a unique ego-alter dyad for each alter, alter attributes are represented, therefore, as a a tie attribute instead.

In a typical study, in which ego-alter dyads are evaluated individually, there are hence two tables linked by ego-ids: one containing ego attributes, the other containing ego-alter tie attributes.

If only summative aspects such as a diversity index of alter attributes or the total strength of ego-alter ties are relevant, the representation can be simplified. Values aggregated over the alteri of each ego can be respresented simply as another ego attribute. The entire data may then consist of ego attributes only. Although the format is then the same as in other population studies, it still originates from relational data and is analyzed from a relational perspective.

Personal Networks

Personal network studies have the same general focus of comparing a population of egos with respect to their social embeddedness. Their data, however, subsume ego network data. In addition to ego and alter attributes and ego-alter tie attributes, they include attributes on alter-alter dyads. Since each alter is affiliated with exactly one ego, and we are only studying dyads between alteri affiliated with the same ego, we are actually studying a collection of complete networks whose boundaries are defined by the alteri of each ego.

To be useful for the comparison of egos, alter attributes will typically be the same for the alteri of different egos. The data are therefore organized into a (global) ego attribute table, a (global) alter attribute table, and one complete network data set per ego.

Hence, and in contrast to ego networks, alter attributes are not represented as attributes of ego-alter ties but rather the other way around. Since alteri in personal network studies are actors in a set of complete networks, they are of interest beyond their affiliation with ego. In fact, the network in which an ego is embedded may contain more actors than are related directly to ego.

3.2 Data Collection

Overlapping dyads as a unit of observation are particular to network studies and require procedures that differ from the collection of attribute data on population samples. Hence, this section focuses on methods for determining the set of dyads on which tie attribute data is collected. For more general introductions to data collection see Lohr (2009), Babbie (2009), or Bernard (2012).

3.2.1 Sources

The initial decision to be made is whether it is necessary to collect data yourself (*primary data*), or whether you can use existing data already compiled by others or yourself, albeit in all but rare cases for a different purpose (*secondary data*).

Primary data can be collected in two ways: *actively* by probing sources of information, i.e., by providing a stimulus to initiate a response from the desired information is inferred, or *passively* by observing a situation without interference.

The main category of active data collection is the survey, and the main categories for passive data collection are observation and archival work.

The delineation is not sharp, since several data collection strategies fall into multiple categories simultaneously. An example would be the compilation of a tailored bibliographic data set using specific queries to multiple databases.

Surveys

Surveys are a form of active data collection and are typically conducted using questionnaires or interviews, where questionnaires can be paper-based or Web-based and interviews can be face-to-face or via the telephone (Fowler 2009).

The most commonly used survey method is the questionnaire. While traditional, paper-based questionnaires are increasingly replaced by Web-based forms, the core aspects relating to networks are still the same. They are used to obtain information on relationships of the respondents themselves or of actors they are assumed to know about. For example, respondents are asked to report on who they give advice to or with whom they share information. Questionnaires can also be used for aggregate actors, such as organizations, by having individual actors representing the collective to provide information on the collective's ties.

The use of questionnaires is not bound to any of the network types, however their design may need to differ accordingly (Marsden 2005). A corresponding questionnaire item usually addresses a specific relation, for example by asking one of the following questions in a free recall design.

With whom do you ...	relation
... talk about problems at work?	professional support
... talk about problems with your kids?	social support
... only exchange professional information?	instrumental

In addition to the mere existence of a relationship, a value indicating a quality or of frequency of interaction may be of interest. Instead of asking which actors in a focal network are connected to each other, researchers might want to find out how intense these relationships are using question such as the following in a free choice design.

How often do you talk to the following?	daily [3]	at least once a week [2]	once or twice per month [1]	less [0]
Alice	☐	☐	☐	☐
Bob	☐	☐	☐	☐
Charlie	☐	☐	☐	☐
⋮				

A most intricate, network-specific decision, however, is the way in which to select dyads that respondents are supposed to evaluate. If they are asked about their own ties, the following are typical design choices.

free choice	alteri are chosen from a given list
rating/ranking	actors from a given list have to be rank-ordered or rated on a given scale
free recall	alteri are chosen unrestrictedly

Each of these designs can be modified by restricting the number of answers sought.

Studies based on choice or rating/ranking need to compile a roster of eligible actors beforehand. This process, during which it is decided who can be a member of the network and who can not, is called *boundary specification* and outlined in more detail in the next section.

A prime example of clearly bounded networks is school classes. Network membership is given, and students can be queried on their friendship ties by asking "Who are your best friends in class?" (e.g., Knecht 2008). This free choice design becomes a *fixed* choice design when the item is rephrased, for instance, as "Who are your five best friends in class?" Fixing the number of answers may provide orientation to respondents as to how to interpret "best," but may also cause them to artificially inflate their response. In a *limited* choice design, the number of answers is not fixed, but an upper or lower bound is set. However, the principle problem remains.

Without a-priori criteria for network membership, the decision as to whom to include may be better left to the respondents. In complete-network studies this raises the question as to whether newly named actors shall also be questioned and if so, where to stop. In a *snowball sample* design, newly named actors are included up to a certain point. This is also addressed in the next section.

Box 13: Newcomb's Fraternity

Social psychologist Theodore M. Newcomb conducted a study on emerging friendship networks in the years 1954–1956 (Newcomb 1961; Nordlie 1958). Its setting is often referred to as "Newcomb's Fraternity." In two consecutive years, 17 male students each were selected from a group of applicants. The selected students were given free lodging in a fraternity. In return they had to participate in 4–5 hours of surveys and discussions every week. During the selection process it was made sure that none of these students had known any of the other students before the experiment. During both years data collection was carried out over the course of 16 weeks with a view to studying the process whereby the students became acquainted with each other. The data included attitudes, popularity, and estimations of attitudes of the other students. Each student had to rate each other student with respect to their "favorableness" once a week on a zero to hundred. They were not allowed to assign a the same score twice in the same week, and responses were actually coded as complete, ordered preference lists.

A classic example combining the above designs is the study by Rapoport and Horvath (1961), in which 861 students of two junior high schools were surveyed. The interest was in connectivity, defined as the fraction of the total population that can be contacted by tracing friendship choices from an arbitrary starting population of nine individuals. Thus the authors asked the students to rank-name their eight best friends in school. They then traced the acquaintance chains created by the student's choices. Note that, even though a roster of eligible actors was given implicitly by the school membership requirement, it was large enough for the design to be regarded as free recall. Recall, on the other hand, was then fixed to a choice of eight who, finally, have to be ranked. Since friends ranked seventh and eighth turned out to be failures significantly more often then those ranked first or second, fixing the number of nominations may have obliged participants to name more friends than they actually had.

An example of a rating/ranking design on the full roster is provided in Box 13.

It is part of the principle of ego-centered network studies that alteri are not known prior to the survey. Since free recall is characterized by a potential bias and recall errors (Borgatti and Molina 2003), a number of approaches to assist and direct free recall have been developed. They are described in detail in Section 3.2.3.

Ego-centered network studies are akin to population studies in that the data sought serves to characterize the focal actors and not a larger structure. When they are conducted in large, open populations, surveying alteri is generally not an option so that the egos must provide information about all relationships and the alteri themselves. Interviews rather than questionnaires can help to increase the willingness of participants, and enable the researcher to react to responses, for example by asking for clarification. On the other hand, this may also result in an interviewer bias.

Observation

The canonical means of passive data collection is observation without intrusion, although participatory observation is common as well.

Observation is particularly helpful when actors are difficult to survey, for example small children, individuals from a different culture, and some types of aggregate actors. Field observation is, therefore, the standard approach in anthropology, in which the interest is in observing regular social situations as they unfold, ideally, without interference and over long periods of time (Bernard 2011; McCurdy, Spradley, and Shandy 2005).

Direct observation and active recording of actions and interactions is increasingly complemented by analysis of digital traces. The exploding use of electronic means of communication is producing a wealth of observational data. Some of this is done purposefully with an analytical objective in mind, some is generated for unknown later use.

More generally, online transaction data such as phone calls, purchase orders, blog postings, wiki edits, or even just search engine use and website browsing are recorded routinely for business, quality control, customization, and marketing. The same is true for credit card payments, bonus card usage, reservations, joint purchase of multiple products, key card access, mobile phone game playing, TV and broadband usage, movement with location-aware devices, and many other everyday activities. At least partial observation of regular social activity has thus become a standard activity, albeit by companies and governments rather than ethnogra-

Box 14: Whyte's Street Corner Society

William F. Whyte, a pioneer in participatory observation, spent three and a half years living in a slum district, almost entirely inhabited by Italian immigrants. In his study "Street Corner Society" (Whyte 1998), he gives an account of his experiences and analyzes the organizational structures of slums and corner gangs. Asked why White chose this particular slum, he answered, "Cornerville best fitted my pictures of what a slum district should look like" (Whyte 1998: 283). "It had more people per acre living in it than any other section of the city. If a slum meant overcrowding, this was certainly it." (Whyte 1998: 283)

The study was time-consuming. That was partly because Whyte had very little background in community study and partly because the topics of interest "... depended upon an intimate familiarity with people and situations" (Whyte 1998: 357). Whyte joined in the local ways of life. For a time he lived with an Italian family, he participated in activities such as bowling, baseball, softball, and cards. He earned the confidence and friendship of the people and became a part of their community.

phers. For businesses and service providers, the statistical analysis of such data is a competitive necessity, and network analysis is part of the toolbox used. Some recorded data is released to the public or, often subject to disclosure conditions, researchers.

Some common differences to survey data and traditional observational data are worth pointing out. Recorded transaction data are very often vast but form an uncontrolled sample. Systematic and technology-induced biases, such as automatic transactions or spam, may require major data cleaning. More generally, the significance of a datum is typically a technical one. An SMS text message is a communication act but its precise content and significance is generally unknown. Similarly, the definition of a Facebook friend is immanent to the system. On the other hand, recorded data are often more convenient and cheaper to collect and there are fewer issues regarding recall, accuracy, or subjectivity.

As with other forms of data collection there are many issues associated with electronically recorded data. We mention two that are of particular relevance for empirical studies. The first major issue is whether the available data is useful for the intended analysis. Because recording is of

Box 15: The Hawthorne Experiments

Roethlisberger and Dickson (1939) analyze the results of a series of inquiries into the effects of work and working conditions at Western Electric Company (Hawthorne Works). The experiences were divided into room studies, interviewing studies, and observational studies. The inspectors selected a vertical section of a department and "... placed the group to be studied in a separate room" (Roethlisberger and Dickson 1939: 387). A room study examined factors in the work place environment that affected worker fatigue. The interviewing studies identified worker attitudes. And through the observation of small work groups, the inspectors collected data about the social relationships and social structure within the group.

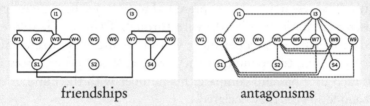

friendships   antagonisms

These two figures show friendships and antagonisms within the bank wiring observation room. The rooms consist of inspectors, wiremen, and soldermen. The first figure shows that friendships tend to cluster in two groups. The second figure shows that antagonism is mainly aimed at people without strong friendships.

limited flexibility, the kinds of observations that are feasible or available as secondary data may not yield data that is useful for the formulation and testing of a hypothesis of interest. The second major issue is ethical. In the majority of cases digital traces are produced by persons who are not aware that they are being observed. Obtaining consent may be challenging to organize and users who are aware of the recording may use a system differently.

A recent study that is highly interesting because it involves many of the aforementioned issues is Bakshy, Rosenn, Marlow, and Adamic (2012).

Box 16: Following and Being Followed

A relation called "following" on Twitter, a microblogging platform, is studied in Huberman, Romero, and Wu (2009). For each user of Twitter the researchers obtained for their data set the number of followers and followees (people followed by a user) the user has declared, along with the content and datestamp of all his/her posts. The data set consisted of a total of 309,740 users, who on average posted 255 posts, had 85 followers, and followed 80 other users. Among the 309,740 users only 211,024 posted at least twice. They call them the active users. They also define the active time of an active user by the time that has elapsed between his first and last post. On average, active users were active for 206 days. The researchers were interested to find out how many people each user communicates directly with through Twitter. Therefore they defined a user's friend as a person at whom the user has directed at least two posts. Using this definition they were able to find out how many friends each user has and compare this number with the number of followers and followees they declared.

Archives

Archival sources can be very useful in passive data collection. They are often the only means of obtaining data about units that are observable in principle, but inaccessible to the researcher. Examples include very large-scale and past networks. Archives are generally inexpensive alternatives, and can also be instrumental in plausibility checking and data completion (see for example Huberman et al. 2009).

Among the many types of archives are libraries, email and calendar entries, church registers, archaeological records, company reports, membership rosters, and all kinds of public, governmental, or commercial databases.

The best-known example of a historic network study is situated in Renaissance Florence (Padgett and Ansell 1993). With data from a multitude of historical records, it is argued that Cosimo de' Medici attained political control by being able to fill structural holes between a number of different political players.

Another example is a study of organizational affiliations of activists in the nineteenth-century women's movement in the USA (Rosenthal, Fingrudt, Ethier, Karant, and McDonald 1985). Similarly, more contemporary studies of interlocking directorates (e.g., Mintz and Schwartz 1985; Burt 1983) derive relations among banks and corporations from board membership records.

Bibliographic databases are an important source for studies in the sociology of science and, despite the many pitfalls, for research performance rankings.

3.2.2 Boundary Specification

Complete networks have a clearly defined boundary separating actors participating in dyads from everyone who does not. This boundary is specified before or during data collection and has been considered the problem of "where to set limits in the analysis of social networks that in reality do not have any obvious limits at all." (Barnes 1979: 414)

Depending on the scenario, there may well be self-evident boundaries. In studies interested in the social structure of bounded groups, such as school classes, business units, or service recipients with a unanimous membership criterion, the boundary is given. This does not imply, however, that members are easy to reach or that surveying or observing them is realistic. It may still be necessary to apply sampling.

In other scenarios it may be difficult to establish a criterion for membership in advance. By overestimating the scope of a network, it remains feasible to adjust an initial boundary by excluding members after data collection.

In surveys that use a choice design, at least, it is difficult to include actors once data collection is underway. Adjustments based on "the relative frequency of interaction, or intensity of ties among members as contrasted with non-members" are common (Wasserman and Faust 1994: 31).

Laumann, Marsden, and Prensky (1989) give a detailed account of the boundary specification problem. They distinguish between the criteria used (actor attributes, relation type, affiliation, or combinations thereof) and the perspective taken (realist or nominalist). Boundary specification from a realist perspective aligns with the perception of the actors. While they may not know each other, they do share the idea of belonging to a definite group such as the alumni of a particular university. Researchers take a nominalist perspective when membership criteria are not those normally applied by the actors themselves as in early adopters of a certain technology.

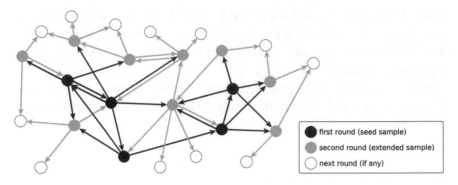

first round (seed sample)

second round (extended sample)

next round (if any)

Figure 12: Two rounds of snowball sampling.

The above examples for initial boundary specification comprise *positional approaches*, in which membership is decided via attributes such as personal characteristics or affiliations with a group. An alternative are *relational approaches*, such as the boundary shrinking described above. The dominant method in this category is *snowball sampling*, during which additional actors are included in a survey if they are nominated in recall items. Criteria for both, that is the inclusion of new actors and stopping the snowball, must be established and clearly communicated. Figure 12 illustrates two waves of snowball sampling on a fictitious network.

Nominations of new actors can be solicited not only via tie-based recall but also by tapping the knowledge that respondents may have about the subject matter. For example, a questionnaire may include a name generating item such as "Which organizations participated in the Iran election protests?" Note that respondents need not be related to these organizations but can help with the implementation of a positional boundary specification.

Clearly, all strategies have advantages and disadvantages. Overly inclusive approaches increase the burden on data collection. However, overly exclusive approaches risk missing actors with an impact on the findings (Mizruchi and Marquis 2006).

Moreover, a researcher might decide to look at participation of specific actor in an incident to answer a research questions such as "Which organizations participated in the Iran election protests?" This event-based strategy is different from formal affiliations and memberships and can help you to identify relevant groups and subjects for your research project. The setting of network boundary is a special problem for complete-network studies. Ego-network studies define the boundary during data collection for example with name generators. We discuss the different forms of data collection for complete and ego networks in the next part of this chapter.

3.2.3 Alter Recall

In a recall design, survey participants are asked to list ties with other actors that may be unknown to the researcher. This is almost always the case in ego-centered network data collection when egos are asked to list alteri but may also be relevant in relational approaches to boundary specification in other network studies.

The corresponding survey items are generally divided into *name generators* and *name interpreters*. With the help of name generators, the respondent is confronted with a specific relation and asked "with whom" he or she is related in this particular way (Diaz-Bone 1997: 52). A name generator defines the boundary of an egocentric network and is, therefore, of central importance for the entire analysis. Generators can be differentiated into *interpersonal* and *global generators* (Pfenning 1995: 46).

Interpersonal name generators relate to a context or a stimulus. Social contexts comprise the interaction spaces of ego and his or her network partners. These include immediate and extended family, the circle of friends, neighbors, colleagues, members of associations, and the broader circle of acquaintances. Individual persons from these social contexts are surveyed. "Crucial for the quality of such applications is the number of the surveyed social contexts" (Pfenning 1995: 47).

The advantage of this surveying method lies in the fact that it takes several spaces of social contact into account and captures most accurately the social environment of the surveyed subjects in terms of completeness. "The interpretation of the individual contexts [...] is problematic (Who is a friend? Who is an acquaintance?) as is the necessity to specify a generalized stimulus (e.g., With whom do you frequently have contact at work? Who are your best three friends?, etc.). This leads to the differentiation between functionally (i.e., also spatially) defined contacts (colleagues, neighbors, and family) and freely selected social relations (friends, acquaintances)." (Pfenning 1995: 47)

Instead of social contexts, stimulus-related interpersonal name generators use specific stimuli, such as shared leisure activities, discussion of important issues, giving of assistance, etc. This helps to avoid deficits and conceptual confusion in the use of social contexts. The biggest methodological problem here lies in the definition of the stimulus specifications. The question as to the centrality of social interactions must be answered in relation to this along with the questions "concerning the completeness of the surveying of the network persons, the fulfillment of the stimulus specifications in accordance with the interaction typology of social interconnectedness, the social web and social network." (Pfenning 1995: 47) It is particularly difficult to capture this information in the case of weak ties as they mostly represent merely situation-related, punctual, and, in many cases, one-off contacts. A long list of very specific interactions is needed to survey such contacts.

Global generators avoid the identification of alteri altogether. In contrast to the context-related name generators, questions about individual persons are not asked here within the specified contexts but "globally or generalized on the basis of the structure of the totality of the relevant social relations." (Pfenning 1995: 47) A survey of this kind could take the form of the ego being asked whether the majority of his or her friends are usually of the same opinion as he or she is, whether most of his or her friends know each other, etc. It is up to the ego him or herself "to carry out and specify a balancing of the individual dyads." (Pfenning 1995: 48) The advantage of this method lies in the almost complete capture of the spaces of social contact. The disadvantage lies in the fact that no dyad-related structural parameters can be calculated and the "personal union" is not controllable (cf. Pfenning 1995: 48). "This lack of selectivity and the balancing of the social relations by the surveyed subject renders this process a particularly subjective form of surveying." (Pfenning 1995: 48)

Once the egocentric network has been delineated, further information is obtained about the persons named by the ego, i.e., the alteri. These additional questions are called *name interpreters*. Generators and interpreters combined are referred to as a *network instrument*.

Name Generators

Burt (1984) developed a network instrument for the General Social Survey (GSS), a national random sample ($n = 1534$) in the USA. It starts with the following name generating question.

> "Q1. From time to time, most people discuss important personal matters with other people. Looking back the last six month – that would be back to last August – who are the people *with whom you discussed an important personal matter*?" (Burt 1984: 331, emphasis in source)

No limit on the number of alteri listed by ego is set. However, if fewer than five alteri are named, interviewers are supposed to probe "anyone else?"

Fourteen subsequent questions are then used as name interpreters. These are applied only to the five persons named first. This restriction is justified with reference to the time taken in the interview to survey the alter-alter relationships as their number grows quadratically with the number of alteri (Burt 1984: 314f).

Question Q2 records whether the ego feels very well acquainted with the alteri, and the persons, with whom the ego feels particularly well acquainted. Question Q3 asks whether the alteri see each other as strangers if they meet on the street, and Q4 asks whether the alteri consider themselves as very well acquainted with each other. Using the following name interpreters, additional information about the alteri is surveyed in relation to gender (Q5), age (Q12), religion (Q13), party preference (Q14), ethnicity (Q6), education (Q7), and income (Q15). Other interpreters specify the surveyed relationship on the basis of the duration of the relationship (Q9), the frequency of contact (Q8), the role assumed by the alter for the ego (Q10), and the topics discussed (Q11).

The use of an instrument for collecting egocentric network data with only one name generator tends to elicit small networks of core ties (Marsden 1987) but "many conceptual understandings of networks extend beyond core ties to include more mundane forms of social support" (Marsden 2005: 12).

An instrument with multiple name generators was designed for the Northern California Community Study (NCCS) (Fischer 1982). It was used in 1977/1978 in a sample stratified by community size in California ($n = 1050$). The Fischer instrument uses ten situation-related or stimulus-related questions on communicative interaction, practical support, and social activities.

The instrument's name generator (Fischer 1982: 315; McCallister and Fischer 1978: 137) includes persons,

1. whom the respondent would ask to look after their house when the respondent is away;
2. with whom the respondent speaks about his or her work;
3. who have helped the respondent with tasks in or around the house in the past three months;
4. with whom the respondent has eaten in the past three months or whom he or she has visited (or by whom he or she has been visited);

5. with whom the respondent sometimes speaks about
   shared leisure activities and hobbies;
6. with whom the unmarried respondent is in a relationship;
7. with whom the respondent speaks about personal matters;
8. whose advice is significant for the respondent in taking important decisions;
9. from whom the respondent would borrow money if he or she needed it
   (if this does not mean that he or she takes out a loan or uses savings);
10. who live in the respondent's household as adults.

Alter-alter relationships are surveyed for up to five alteri. Generators (1), (4), (5), and (7)–(9) are used here for the compilation of a list of these alteri. The first persons surveyed by these generators are listed in each case. Persons from the respondent's household and persons already listed are passed over (Fischer 1982: 332). The ego is then asked whether the listed persons know each other well. The age-age relationships are recorded by the Fisher instrument using this interpreter. At the end of the interview, a second and more comprehensive list is compiled of all persons named by the informant in the course of the interview for all ten generators. The respondent is then asked whether the list is complete or whether a person who is important to him or her is missing. Using name interpreters, the role relationship of the alter for the ego (the specified roles are: relation, colleague, neighbor, friend, acquaintance, other) and the gender of the alter are surveyed for all of the persons on the list. The intimacy of the relationship, the distance between homes (up to five minutes by car, more than one hour away), the availability of a meeting place (café, park or other) that can be reached within five minutes, the similarities between the ego and the alteri in terms of profession, ethnicity or nationality, religion, and the (leisure) activities pursued are also recorded. As is the case with the Burt instrument, the relationships between the alteri are also surveyed using the Fischer instrument for five people named by the ego. Because the structure of the surveyed egocentric network is only known for a partial network, this partial network is also referred to as a "small Fischer network."

Position Generators

Rather than identifying particular alteri using name generators, a position generator measures linkages to specific locations. This instrument has proven particularly useful for investigations of the productivity of general individual social capital, i.e., social capital research about general populations that does not focus on a particular life domain.

Lin (2001) assumes that access resources arise through embeddedness in a social structure that can be mobilized in a targeted way. He describes these resources as social capital. There are two methods for measuring such resources: first, the use of interpersonal name generators and, second, the position generator.

Lin states that name generators are insufficient as, by definition, they are linked to content unless there is information available about the population or content of the universe (roles, familiarity, geography, etc.). Hence, Lin proposes a different measurement instrument which he developed: the position generator. According to Lin, the position generator measures the access to network members via their professional position, which is understood as an existing social resource based on the prestige of the job in question within a hierarchically organized social structure. This instrument is not exactly easy to use but it is efficient. Using this instrument, different basic entities can be studied in a differentiated way. It is based on a clear theoretical foundation (distribution of prestige which can be referred back to, highest access prestige, and the number of accesses to different positions). In addition to positions, respondents identify relationship types (family, friend, acquaintance) for each accessed position.

Lin, Fu, and Hsung (2001) applied the position generator shown in Figure 13 to studies carried out in Taiwan. They also asked (Lin et al. 2001: 69) about the number of daily contacts

> In an ordinary day, how many people are you roughly in contact with?
> □ 0–4   □ 5–9   □ 10–19   □ 20–49   □ 100 or more

and how well the respondents knew these persons ("1. Know almost all of them; 2. Know most of them; 3. About half and half; 4. Don't know most of them; 5. Know almost none of them"). A value was created from these data which indicated that the higher the value, the less familiar the respondent is with his daily contacts. This corresponds to Granovetter's theory of the strength of weak ties, i.e., that extensive, less familiar contacts enlarge the networks and provide better access to social capital.

Resource Generators

Another instrument for the measurement of individual social capital in volves tapping resources rather than context or positions (van der Gaag and Snijders 2005). This instrument also differs from other measurement instruments for social capital; it does not include the mapping of an ego-centered network (as with the use of name generators), instead it bears

Q1. Among your relatives, friends, or acquaintances, are there people who have the following jobs?

Q2. If so, what his/her relationship to you?

Q3. If you don't know anyone with these jobs, and if you need to find such a person for private help or to ask about same problems, who among those you know would you go through to fin such a person? Who would he/she be to you?

Q4. What jobs does he/she do?

(see Q1–Q4 above)	Q1 1. Yes 2. No	Q2 see list below	Q3 see list below	Q4 see list below
a. High school lecturer				
b. Electrician				
c. Owner of small factory/firm				
d. Nurse				
e. Assemblymen/women at provincial or city/county level				
f. Truck driver				
g. Physician				
h. Manager of large factory/firm				
i. Police (regular policeman)				
j. Head of division, county/city government				
k. Housemaid or cleaning worker				
l. Reporter				
m. Owner of big factory/firm				
n. Lawyer				
o. Office workman or guard				

Figure 13: Generator based on positions (Lin 2001).

more similarity to the position generator (Lin and Dumin 1986). It differs from the position generator, in particular, by referring directly to accessed social resources rather than occupational prestige. Whereas the position generator can be used to measure access to social resources useful in instrumental actions, the information retrieved by the resource generator can refer more clearly to social resources useful in expressive actions.

The structure of the resource generator is the same as that of the position generator and shown in Figure 14. However, a defined list of resources is used here which encompass the concrete sub-resources of social capital and hence render the respondents' access to resources visible. As with the position generator, in addition to the resources, the strength of a relationship, relationship type (family member, friend, or acquaintance),

Do you know anyone who...	Acquaintance	Friend	Family member
1. can repair a car, bike etc.	☐	☐	☐
2. owns a car	☐	☐	☐
3. is handy repairing household equipment	☐	☐	☐
4. can speak an write a foreign language	☐	☐	☐
5. can work with a personal computer	☐	☐	☐
6. can play an instrument	☐	☐	☐
7. has knowledge of literature	☐	☐	☐
8. has senior high school (VWO) education	☐	☐	☐
9. has higher vocational (HBO) education	☐	☐	☐
10. reads a professional journal	☐	☐	☐
11. is active in a political party	☐	☐	☐
12. owns shares for at least Dfl. 10,000	☐	☐	☐
13. works at the town hall	☐	☐	☐
14. earns more than Dfl: 5,000 monthly	☐	☐	☐
15. owns a holiday home abroad	☐	☐	☐
16. sometimes has the opportunity to hire people	☐	☐	☐
17. knows a lot about governmental regulations	☐	☐	☐
18. has good contacts with a newspaper, radio or TV station	☐	☐	☐
19. knows about soccer	☐	☐	☐
20. has knowledge about financial matters (taxes, subsidies)	☐	☐	☐
21. can find a holiday job for a family member	☐	☐	☐
22. can give advice concerning a conflict at work	☐	☐	☐
23. can help when moving house (packing, lifting)	☐	☐	☐
24. can help with small jobs around the house	☐	☐	☐
25. can do you shopping when you are ill	☐	☐	☐
26. can give medical advice, when you are dissatisfied with your doctor	☐	☐	☐
27. can lend you a large sum of money (Dfl. 10,000)	☐	☐	☐
28. can provide a place to stay if you have to leave your house temporarily	☐	☐	☐
29. can give advice concerning a conflict with family members	☐	☐	☐
30. can discuss what political party you are going to vote for	☐	☐	☐
31. can give advice on matters law	☐	☐	☐
32. can give a good reference when you are applying for a job	☐	☐	☐
33. can babysit for your children	☐	☐	☐

Figure 14: Generator based on resources (van der Gaag and Snijders 2005).

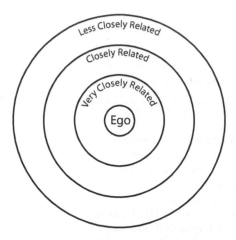

Figure 15: Network card (Kahn and Antonucci 1980).

etc. are also recorded. In this case also, it is not possible to eliminate incompatibility problems arising from its use in different contexts as the list of specific resources makes a series of variation possibilities in different contexts possible. Hence the composition of the instrument depends on the systematic, theoretical consideration which represent social resources, i.e., the "general social capital" of individuals.

Network Maps

Kahn and Antonucci (1980) describe procedures for identifying providers of social support, using both affective and role relation name generators and concentric circle diagrams for listing network members in relation to a respondent.

This instrument is particularly suited to the recording of the emotional proximity and importance of persons in a network. Like the other generators discussed in this section, it is also particularly suited for surveying egocentric networks, in which little is known about the field in which the respondents operate, e.g., immigrants. The respondent is presented with the diagram shown in Figure 15, which consists of three concentric circles. Ego, the respondent, is made the focal actor in the innermost circle. The respondents are asked to enter names or initials of those persons, to whom they feel emotionally connected or who are important to them personally in the three circles. The persons to whom they feel closest and who are most important to them are entered in the innermost circle. De-

	incomplete	inaccurate	inconsistent
causes	non-response data loss	poor design error	perception intention
	⋮	⋮	⋮
effect	missing information	misleading information	contradictory or complementary information

Figure 16: Data quality issues.

pending on the information required, attribute data, such as age, gender, nature of relationship (family, friend, colleague, etc.), duration of the relationship, frequency of contact, etc. can then be surveyed for all of the persons entered in the circles.

3.3 Quality Issues

Data will never be perfect. In most cases it will not even describe exactly what is needed to answer a research question but only related phenomena that are observed or represented more easily. Even if it did provide such answers, lack of access, measurement error, transcription, and numerous other factors will inevitably cause quality impairments.

Hence, it is important to be aware of the types of quality issues that you may encounter. Knowing about them and some of their possible sources is more helpful than a series of dos and don'ts as it will help you to maintain a critical attitude towards the significance of patterns in the data and computational results.

Instead of going through a list of possible sources of error, or how to avoid them, we have organized this section according to the type of problem and its consequences. An overview is provided in Figure 16.

Incomplete Data

Missing data (Little and Rubin 1989; Allison 2001; Little and Schenker 1995) is always a nuisance because, by definition, an attempt was made to collect the data but it was not available to the researcher. Possible causes of missing network data (Kossinets 2006) include the misspecification of network boundaries, inaccessibility, non-response, drop-out (in longitudinal studies), data loss, and many more. Of course, you should always try to obtain data as completely as possible; if this were not necessary, you would be looking for the wrong data in the first place.

Whether missing data affect your conclusions depends on

- how much data are missing,
- which data are missing, and
- how they became missing.

For instance, a study hypothesizing that the degree of social support received is negatively related to income may fail to find an association if high-income respondents are less likely to report it. This is an example of a systematic bias and called *missing at random* because it is conceivable that other attributes, such as level of education, are also related to income, and may, therefore, be helpful in *imputing* plausible values for the missing ones without distorting the results. Since priors were drafted in a lottery, for instance, the three values missing in Figure 7 could be imputed quite reasonably by distributing the number of seats not covered by the other families according to the number of family members eligible at the times.

Imputation of network data (Robins, Pattison, and Woolcock 2004) has not yet been applied extensively although there is a growing body of literature on predicting unobserved or future relationships (Liben-Nowell and Kleinberg 2007).

One extreme case in which there is no underlying systematic bias is called *missing completely at random*. In population samples this can often be dealt with by ignoring missing data because the assumption implies that the only consequence is a reduced sample size. While this approach may also apply to ego network studies, it is almost certain to fail in complete-network studies because of the inherent dependencies of overlapping dyads and the frequent use of indirect relations in analyses. Even if some studies suggest concrete numbers, such as an 80 percent response rate, above which, for example, the identification of the most central actors becomes reliable, we recommend that you do not apply them. At best, they are rules of thumb that are useful across a large number of studies with incomplete data sets of similar type. Your study is likely to be dealing with only a few networks, and most network-analytic techniques are very sensitive to even small changes in the data. Simply compare a ring-like structure and a chain of links: A single missing relationship makes all the difference for the actors at the ends of the chain.

At the other extreme, the bias is again systematic, however, dependencies are not with respect to any of the observed data. This is called *missing not at random* and the toughest problem to deal with. The potential for this to arise can at least be reduced sometimes by introducing additional attributes into the design of a study.

Inaccurate Data

Data are *inaccurate* if they are not missing but comprised of values that deviate from the intended ones. Sources of inaccuracy include measurement error, informant lack of recall, intentional lying, and many others.

Active data collection methods are highly dependent on the willingness and capacity of respondents to provide accurate information. Inaccuracy is particularly common when respondents have a different understanding of the definition of a relationship. This once again highlights the need for the precise and comprehensible formulation of questionnaire items. Are you sure that the respondents understand what they are supposed to answer? Do they have appropriate options? Can they reasonably be expected to know this information? Even in the given situation?

While in most cases we know when values are missing, it is difficult to assess when they are accurate (Butts 2003). Inaccuracy may be systematic or random. Data generation processes that consistently produce the same information (possibly from different angles) are called *reliable*, irrespective of whether the information in question is accurate or subject to systematic error. If the information is generally accurate but perturbed by random error, the process is referred to as *valid*.

Hence, both reliability and validity are necessary to obtain accurate data. The implementation of data collection methods according to these criteria may depend on the analytic interest, however. For example, Pfenning (1995) compares the reliability of Burt and Fisher's instruments, which are described above, with respect to the properties of the resulting ego networks. Because of the larger number of stimuli, Fischer's instrument generates more consistent alter lists. In a test-retest approach, 63 percent of alteri were named in both tests using Fischer's instrument, compared to 45 percent for Burt's. While this resulted in a more reliable heterogeneity indicator, a size indicator varied more strongly than with Burt's instrument.

Inconsistent Data

We say that data are *inconsistent* if variables supposed to represent the same information have different values. This includes the case in which one of them is missing. Sources of inconsistent data include repeated or alternative measurements of the same property, the mismatch of a set of particular values and their supposed aggregate, impossible values, and many more.

Bernard, Killworth, and Sailer (1980; 1982); Bernard, Johnson, Killworth, Kronenfeld, and Sailer (1985) observed social interactions within several different groups (students, managers, radio amateurs, a group of blind people, and employees of a social research institute) and then asked members of these groups about their relationships. As it turns out, just about half of the ties named by the respondents matched the observed ones. These studies have inspired further research with similar questions (Hammer 1985; Freeman and Romney 1987; Freeman, Romney, and Freeman 1987). An important conclusion for network research is that the recall of social interactions appears to be governed more by an underlying cognitive structure than by the actual short-term interactions. As a consequence, observed interactions may not be indicative of the more stable, longer-term relations in a group.

Another common case of inconsistent data is encountered when actors are asked to self-report relationships that exist between them. Since every relationship is assessed twice, once by each actor in the dyad, this is bound to lead to disagreement, even for relations that may appear indisputable to a researcher. If it is not possible to repeat the questioning, the data is frequently recoded by aggregating the two responses into one. For non-valued relations, the two main options are to treat an unconfirmed relationship as either

- absent (*minimum symmetrization*) or
- present (*maximum symmetrization*).

The term *symmetrization* derives from undirected relations in which responses can be seen as an asymmetric generalization of the relation. Neither is particularly satisfying because we either lose or impute data based on the understanding that there is a true situation that at least one of the respondents describes inaccurately. It may be more appropriate, however, to embrace the inconsistency and analyze whether the disagreement is actually informative in terms of the different perceptions of a relationship that actors may have.

An extreme case of this view underlies the concept of cognitive social structures. Actors assess every relationship not necessarily to arrive at a better consensus value but to investigate different cognitive models and how they relate to network behavior.

3.4 Ethical Considerations

Ethical considerations play an important role in all stages of a network study.

For example, during the early research design phase, you should consider the degree of intrusion imposed on the subjects while collecting network data from them: Indirect observation of subjects' behavior is less intrusive than interviews and surveys directly collected from the subjects, however, it may also be perceived as voyeuristic.

In the later stages of a network study, data storage and the protection of privacy should be considered carefully. Decisions regarding the way, in which findings are reported and possible implications discussed with the subjects need to be made towards the end of the project.

Many research institutions require researchers to comply with their internal ethics guidelines for research involving human subjects. While we recognize that there are differing international practices, we would like to highlight the importance of the elements that constitute the institutional review process before researchers start to collect and analyze network data.

First, researchers need to inform their subjects that the questions are not designed to cause harm to their position when they participate in the research study. This form of human subject protection is called informed consent, and most internal review boards require subjects to sign a form confirming that they understand the potential risks of revealing their network relationships. The process is necessary to ensure that individual rights are protected and that the study is ethically appropriate and may proceed (Klovdahl 2005). Borgatti and Molina (2003) highlights the importance of subject protection so that researchers do not compromise the successful approval of future network studies.

One of the main tensions in network research is that network data cannot be anonymous: Instead, both the respondents and their contact names must be known to the researcher to enable the collection of data and conduct of the analysis. In addition, the respondents and their nominated contacts must be identifiable to match attributes, such as gender, political affiliations, etc. to them and their relationships. This means that network data cannot be independent and this creates significant responsibilities for researchers (Breiger 2005).

Another ethical consideration already addressed earlier in this chapter concerns decisions about the inclusion or exclusion of network actors. As soon as the researcher imposes an artificial boundary around the perceived network, he or she includes or excludes actors that may or may not have to be included. Connected to this is the decision on how to handle non-respondents: Are they still considered to be part of the network because they were mentioned by other actors in the network? Or, do they need to be removed from the data analysis because they themselves opted out of participating in the data collection? Kadushin (2005) suggests that every researcher must make the best possible assessment as to how the network data may be used, particularly in the case of military or public health networks.

When all of the data have been collected, you will be confronted with decisions on how to handle the data and protect the confidentiality of the responses and anonymity of subjects (Borgatti and Molina 2005).

One way to ensure the confidentiality of the responses is the assignment of id numbers to each subject (which we recommend anyway, see above) and removal of all other identifiers from the data. This way individuals are less likely to be identified, although it must be considered that their specific role or position in the social structure may expose them any way. This stresses once again that data on overlapping dyads may be heavily interdependent.

Another way to ensure subject anonymity is to display and publish only aggregated network data so that roles and positions cannot be identified even by those who know the context or are represented in it. We also recommend that this practice be adopted when researchers discuss their findings with potential clients. We consider this an important practice to protect participants from facing potentially negative ramifications.

A more comprehensive overview of the question of ethics may be obtained from the special issue of the journal *Social Networks* entitled "Ethical dilemmas in social network research."[1]

---

1 *Social Networks 27* (2), 2005.

3.5 Summary

A prerequisite for empirical hypothesis testing is the availability of suitable data. Network studies generally involve data for two types of observational units, actors, and dyads. The latter are the main characteristic of network studies. Because data defined on dyads is indexed by two actors rather than one, data tables need to be adapted accordingly.

We have distinguished primary data collected by yourself from secondary data that are already available. Secondary data are mostly collected by previous studies or extracted from databases and archives. Typical strategies for primary data collection are surveys (questionnaires, interviews, etc.) and observation (field observation, electronic transaction recording, etc.). In general, surveying is a form of active data collection in which a response is elicited by providing stimuli such as questionnaire items, whil observing is a form of passive data collection in which regular behavior is recorded.

Ideally, the decision for any of these strategies depends exclusively on the data that would concur with your research question. In many cases, a compromise must be made because the desired data may be impossible or too costly to obtain.

For primary data collection, the crucial decision concerns which actors to include. In ego-centered network studies this amounts to deciding on the population of focal actors and a sampling strategy. It is thus akin to other population sampling approaches. For complete networks, however, the population coincides with the actors of the network. It must, therefore, be bounded more restrictively, either by defining the boundary explicitly (and possibly narrowing it later on) or by expanding the network during data collection as in snowball sampling.

We also discussed several instruments for network surveys in detail. These use various techniques for assisting respondents to recall actors, to whom they are related in a given way. While they are primarily used in ego-centered network studies, similar techniques are useful in snowball sampling.

As usual, actor and tie attributes may require cleaning, filtering, normalization, and other kinds of preparatory transformation. While this may be inherent in the design of the data collection process, it may also be triggered by data quality issues. In this context, we differentiated between incomplete (missing), inaccurate (unreliable or invalid), and inconsistent (inaccurate or more fine-grained) data. A special transformation is anonymization which is merely one technique for dealing with ethical issues such as privacy.

3.6 Exercises

1. For a network study on status and reputation of developers in an open-source software project, assume that you can obtain data on the assignment of developers to reported bugs.

   – What are the units of observation?

   – Is this active or passive data collection?

   – Are these primary or secondary data?

   – How would you organize the data? Why?

2. Explain the difference between a monadic and a dyadic variable to a friend or colleague.

3. Given a network of 1024 actors with 4211 ties, how many cells does the actor-by-actor table have? Compare this to the number of entries in a tie-by-attribute table and an actor-by-ties list.

4. What defines the boundary of a network?

5. Mobile phone service providers are interested in understanding which conditions prompt customers to terminate their calling plans (i.e., in predicting churn). It is assumed that calling patterns and churn of important calling partners are relevant indicators.

   – Outline a data collection strategy for a personal-network survey.

   – What if you can gain access to a provider's contract and call data?

6. Suppose you are planning to survey candidates for committee positions in a political party regarding their allies and competitors among all party members.

   – Formulate survey items for these relations.

   – How are you going to determine network boundaries?

   – Are there ethical considerations to address?

7. Describe and compare the data that is obtained from interviews using network maps or resource generators.

8. Discuss the differences between face-to-face interviews and online surveys. What are implications of these differences for the data obtained via one of the instruments described in this chapter?

9. Invent a scenario in which inconsistent data is more informative than data corrected for consistency.

4 Analysis

You will now learn about methods that help to make sense of network data. There are two essential steps here: first, the specific functioning of a network is represented in a dyad index that assesses the direct and indirect relations between pairs of actors; second, such dyad indices are used to identify influential positions (centrality) and groups of cohesive (clustering) or similar (roles) actors. In addition, we will take a brief look at models of networks that can be used to explain or predict structural features, also in relation to actor attributes.

Having collected and stored data on the phenomenon of interest, we are ready to make sense of it.

Generally speaking, the purpose of analysis is to extract from input data information that can be used to describe, explain, or predict situations or developments. In principle, there is nothing special about *network* data analysis as, like other statistical analyses, it merely involves the attempt to make distinctions and find associations between quantities. The difference, however, lies in the definition (and thus computation) of the quantities involved. Since networks yield relational data, concepts that differ from those used in the analysis of conventional data tables are available—and required.

This chapter provides a structured overview of the formal toolbox of network analysis (Brandes and Erlebach 2005). While details are provided for the most commonly applied methods, information is also provided on where to look for additional methods, should they be required for a particular study.

Our basic data format is a single network of actors who may have additional attributes. Many methods extend to more general situations, however. Although not entirely accurate, the following linkage between tasks and methods provides a reasonable initial approximation and may serve as a guide through this chapter.

Description: The structure of networks can be summarized using various indicators that frequently constitute quantitative assessments of variance in the structural positions of actors and their composition. Beyond their descriptive function, such indicators are often related to other quantities when the objective is to spot network effects or determinants.

Explanation: The structure of observed networks is commonly explained using network formation models. This is done, for example, by devising a generative model that yields networks with structural characteristics similar to the observed networks, or by fitting a parametric model to an observation.

Prediction: If only determining factors such as a preceding network configuration are known, one way to predict the formation or evolution of a network is simulation. Simulation, like fitting, is a specific use of network models.

Network data types are described in more detail in the following section; the subsequent sections are organized according to analytical interests.

It should be noted that we do not distinguish between complete and ego network analysis in this chapter because most methods are relevant to both cases. In fact, the most important differences do not show up during evaluation but during data collection and interpretation. Nevertheless, it should be noted that the methods most relevant for ego network analysis are network characteristics as described in Section 4.2.2.

4.1   Mathematical Representation

This chapter appears to be more formal than previous ones because of its more extensive use of mathematical symbols and formulas. If you are not familiar with symbolic notation, please observe that it is not only used for the purpose of brevity, it often offers a convenient way of attaining an appropriate level of precision. While many books attempt to provide less mathematical treatments, these often result in long-winded and more complicated verbal statements that ultimately generate greater confusion because it is difficult to avoid ambiguity using natural language. Note also

Box 17: Some Mathematical Notation

Symbol $\in$ is shorthand notation for "contained in," i.e., $x \in S$ denotes that x is an element in set S. For two sets S and T, $S \subseteq T$ indicates that every element of S is also an element of T, i.e., S is a subset of T. Similarly, $S_1 \cup S_2$ and $S_1 \cap S_2$ denote the union and intersection of sets S_1, S_2. The number of elements in a set S, i.e., the set's cardinality, is denoted by $|S|$.

The sum over all elements x of a set S is abbreviated as $\sum_{x \in S} x$. The binomial coefficient $\binom{n}{k} = \frac{n!}{k!(n-k)!}$ gives the number of k-element subsets of a set with n elements, where $n! = n \cdot (n-1) \cdot \ldots \cdot 2 \cdot 1$ denotes the nth factorial.

For a range of values R, $R^{n \times m}$ denotes the set of all matrices with n rows, m columns, and entries from R.

The type of a function f is declared as $f : D \to R$, meaning that f maps elements from a domain D to values in a range R.

that, although we use symbolic notation for clarity, we do not practice mathematical derivations.

In previous chapters, we used graphical and matrix notations to represent the structure of a network. For many of the methods introduced in this chapter, it is more convenient to use the combinatorial representation of a graph defined below.

The matrix representation may be most familiar to you as this is how network data is entered into spreadsheets. Each cell is indexed by a row index and a column index. If both rows and columns are labeled with actors of a (one-mode) network, the matrix is square and each cell can be referenced by specifying a row actor i and a column actor j. The corresponding cell content, a_{ij}, describes the relationship between i and j. For a non-valued relation, i.e., one that is either present or absent, the conventional choice is $a_{ij} = 1$ if the relation is present, and $a_{ij} = 0$ otherwise. Two-mode networks yield rectangular matrices, in which the rows and columns are labeled with the elements of the two distinct modes, however, the meaning of an entry is analogous.

For one-mode networks there is a second entry, a_{ji}, indexed by the same two actors but in the opposite order. If the relation coded in a matrix is symmetric, as in being friends, then all pairs of entries a_{ij} and a_{ji}

graphical	matrix	graph
$i \bullet \qquad \bullet j$	$a_{ij} = 0,\, a_{ji} = 0$	$(i,j) \notin E,\, (j,i) \notin E$ resp. $\{i,j\} \notin E$
$i \bullet\!\longrightarrow\!\bullet j$	$a_{ij} = 1,\, a_{ji} = 0$	$(i,j) \in E,\, (j,i) \notin E$
$i \bullet\!\longleftarrow\!\bullet j$	$a_{ij} = 0,\, a_{ji} = 1$	$(i,j) \notin E,\, (j,i) \in E$
$i \bullet\!\rightleftarrows\!\bullet j$ or $\quad i \bullet\!\longrightarrow\!\bullet j$	$a_{ij} = 1,\, a_{ji} = 1$	$(i,j) \in E,\, (j,i) \in E$ resp. $\{i,j\} \in E$

Figure 17: Equivalent representations of the four possible dyad configurations in an ordered (or unordered) boolean relation.

will be equal. The coding is thus redundant and the matrix is also referred to as symmetric. This need not be the case if the relation is potentially asymmetric, as in one actor considering the other to be a friend. For a non-valued relation this yields the four possible combinations, two symmetric and two asymmetric ones, for every pair of actors. We refer to a pair of actors such as i and j, irrespective of their relation, as a *dyad*. By convention, potentially asymmetric relations are coded in such a way that they extend from the row actor to the column actor. The four possible configurations thus suggest the graphical notation depicted in Figure 17.

4.1.1　Graphs

Matrix representations are useful for data management and certain calculations, and graphical representations are a convenient means of communication. For most of the structural considerations that we will be dealing with in this chapter, however, the combinatorial representation of a graph is more appropriate.

A *graph* G is a pair $G = (V, E)$ that consists of a set V of *vertices*, and a set E of *edges*. While the elements of V represent the actors of the network, the ties between them are represented in E. Therefore, an edge is simply a pair of vertices, however, since the relation may be potentially asymmetric, the pair may have to be ordered. Hence, if the relation between a pair of vertices $i, j \in V$ is potentially asymmetric, the order of i and j in the pair is used to resolve potential ambiguities analogous to the matrix entries. In this case we say that the edges are *directed* and de-

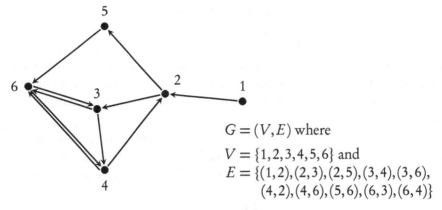

$G = (V, E)$ where

$V = \{1, 2, 3, 4, 5, 6\}$ and

$E = \{(1,2), (2,3), (2,5), (3,4), (3,6),$
$(4,2), (4,6), (5,6), (6,3), (6,4)\}$

Figure 18: A graph with $n = 6$ vertices, $m = 10$ directed edges, and $6 \cdot 5/2 = 15$ dyads.

note them using parentheses $(i, j) \in E$. Directed edges are thus a subset $E \subseteq V \times V = \{(i, j) : i, j \in V\}$ of all possible pairs of vertices, where pairs (i, j) and (j, i) are considered to be different edges corresponding to the two matrix entries a_{ij} and a_{ji} if $i \neq j$. Otherwise, edges are referred to as *undirected* and denoted using curly braces $\{i, j\} \in E$. The set notation indicates that $\{i, j\}$ and $\{j, i\}$ denote the same edge.

Since every undirected edge is represented equivalently by two directed edges (one for each ordering), directed graphs are more general. For most purposes in this chapter, an undirected graph can be thought of as a symmetric directed graph. If not stated otherwise, we assume in this chapter that edges are directed, although it should be noted that most definitions apply analoguously to undirected (symmetric) relations. Also, we assume that there are no *loops* (i, i) connecting a vertex $i \in V$ with itself, i.e., no diagonal elements in the matrix representation.

We will use $n = |V|$ to denote the number of vertices, and $m = |E|$ to denote the number of edges throughout.

The set of all dyads in a graph $G = (V, E)$ is $D(G) = \{\{i, j\} : i \neq j \in V\}$. Consequently, a graph with n vertices has $\binom{n}{2} = \frac{n(n-1)}{2}$ dyads. In an undirected graph without loops, there can be at most one edge per dyad, so that $E \subseteq D(G)$ and thus $m \leq \frac{n(n-1)}{2}$. In a directed graph without loops, there can be two edges per dyad (one in each direction), so that $m \leq n(n-1)$. In either case, the number of edges is at most quadratic in the number of vertices.

Just as numbers are abstracted from the objects being counted to allow for more general statements about quantities, vertices and edges are abstracted from actors and their ties to allow for more general statements about structures. It should be noted, however, that all other information specific to these entities is ignored deliberately. If vertices or edges represent qualitatively different actors or ties, vertex or edge attributes are needed for differentiation.

There is a straightforward correspondence between matrix and graph representations. The type of matrix we have been using so far has $n \times n$ entries and is called the *adjacency matrix* $A(G) = (a_{ij})_{i,j \in V}$ of G, where

$$a_{ij} = \begin{cases} 1 & \text{if } (i,j) \in E \\ 0 & \text{otherwise} . \end{cases}$$

An alternative representation based on membership of actors in dyads is the $n \times m$ *incidence matrix* $B(G) = (b_{ie})_{i \in V, e \in E}$ with

$$b_{ie} = \begin{cases} 1 & \text{if } e = (i,j) \in E \text{ for some } j \in V \\ -1 & \text{if } e = (j,i) \in E \text{ for some } j \in V \\ 0 & \text{otherwise} . \end{cases}$$

In an incidence matrix, each column has two entries, because every column corresponds to one edge, and the sign indicates its direction. Since symmetric relations would yield two columns per dyad that differ only in their signs, undirected graphs are frequently represented with one column per edge and no signs, i.e., entries are either 0 or 1, but not -1.

Please note that relations involving more than two actors can be represented in an incidence matrix but not in an adjacency matrix. This becomes more obvious when incidence matrices are interpreted as *two-mode* matrices, in which actors are the row-mode and their relations the column-mode. Two-mode networks are introduced in Section 4.1.3 below.

A graph $G' = (V', E')$ is a *subgraph* of a graph $G = (V, E)$, $G' \subseteq G$, if $V' \subseteq V$ and $E' \subseteq E$. Note that G' is required to be a graph, i.e., we can only have those edges in E' that connect vertices present in V'. By $G[V']$ we denote the unique *vertex-induced* subgraph of G that contains the vertices in V' and all edges that connect vertices of V' in G. Likewise, the *edge-induced* subgraph $G[E']$ contains the edges in E' and precisely those vertices that are incident to any edge of E' in G.

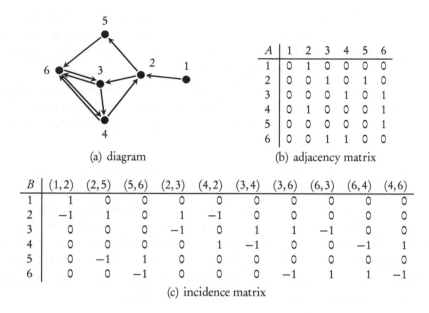

A	1	2	3	4	5	6
1	0	1	0	0	0	0
2	0	0	1	0	1	0
3	0	0	0	1	0	1
4	0	1	0	0	0	1
5	0	0	0	0	0	1
6	0	0	1	1	0	0

(a) diagram   (b) adjacency matrix

B	(1,2)	(2,5)	(5,6)	(2,3)	(4,2)	(3,4)	(3,6)	(6,3)	(6,4)	(4,6)
1	1	0	0	0	0	0	0	0	0	0
2	−1	1	0	1	−1	0	0	0	0	0
3	0	0	0	−1	0	1	1	−1	0	0
4	0	0	0	0	1	−1	0	0	−1	1
5	0	−1	1	0	0	0	0	0	0	0
6	0	0	−1	0	0	0	−1	1	1	−1

(c) incidence matrix

Figure 19: Three alternative representations of the same graph.

4.1.2 Ego-Centered Networks

As discussed in Chapter 2, ego-centered networks comprise a mixture of network and population studies as a population of actors (the *egos*) is studied in terms of their (individual) social embeddings and not in terms of the relations between them. However, their embeddings are captured by relations with and between other actors (the *alteri*) on a per-ego basis.

Depending on the specific data available about the environment of each ego, ego networks require different representations. The following are typical scenarios (cf. also Section 3.1.3):

- The embedding of a person in his or her social environment is described by a collection of numerical or categorical values. While these values may characterize the network among alteri, it is possible that this network was never determined explictly because the values were surveyed directly. For example, the respondents may have been asked to rate the diversity of their personal networks without providing any details about it. Either way, there is no graph involved in the subsequent analyses.

- Knowing the relationship of ego to some alteri, but not those among alteri, yields the intermediate case of ego networks consisting only of ego-alter dyads. Although these form a (star-like) graph, they are usually represented as a list of ego attributes.
- If data about the relationships between alteri is available, the resulting personal networks can be treated like any other complete network. In this case, the relationships between ego and each alter are best represented in an alter attribute.

Despite the fact that the first two scenarios are grounded in a structural perspective, in general, the data analyzed are not relational. From a technical point of view, ego network studies using such data are more akin to population statistics. In the third scenario, however, genuine relational data is observed, if only between ego and alteri as well as between alteri but not among egos. When a collection of networks based on the same type of relation consisting of one network per ego is obtained, they are sometimes referred to as a *personal network ensemble*.

4.1.3   Two-Mode Networks

Sometimes the relation between actors is, in fact, established indirectly via entities that are not considered as actors in the same sense. In studies of interlocking directorates, for instance, relations between directors are derived from joint board memberships, i.e., from relations involving two types of entities, directors and boards.

Networks consisting of two categorically different types of entities and a relation involving one member of each type are called *two-mode networks*. As discussed in Chapter 3, they can be represented in rectangular matrices $B \in \{0,1\}^{n \times m}$ in which one type of entity (e.g., actors) indexes the n rows, and the other type (e.g., social settings) indexes the m columns. Let an entry b_{ie} in that matrix be 1, if entity i of one type is tied to entity e of the other type, and 0 otherwise. Matrices of two-mode networks then generalize regular incidence matrices to the case of *undirected hypergraphs* because a column corresponds to a (hyper)edge, which can have any number of incident vertices rather than just two.

The analytical procedures available for two-mode networks (Freeman and White 1993; Faust 1997; Borgatti and Everett 1997; Doreian, Batagelj, and Ferligoj 2004) are less developed than those available for single-mode networks. Therefore, two-mode networks are often transformed into weighted undirected graphs via an operation called *projection*. Projection to the row-mode or column-mode yields adjacency matrices

$$A^{row} = BB^T \quad \text{or} \quad A^{col} = B^T B \,,$$

where B^T is the matrix *transpose* of B in which row and column indices are swapped, i.e., the entries are related by $b_{ij}^T = b_{ji}$. Hence, an entry $a_{ij}^{row} = \sum_{e=1}^{m} b_{ie} b_{ej}^T = \sum_{e=1}^{m} b_{ie} b_{je}$ of the $n \times n$ row-mode projection corresponds to the number of entries that rows i and j of B have in common.

Projection to the row-mode or column-mode is generally irreversible because several different two-mode networks may yield the same projection. Whenever possible, you should try to operate on the two-mode data directly, also because projections tend to be dense and thus more computationally demanding in subsequent analyses. This is because every entity of degree d in one mode induces a complete subgraph of d vertices (and thus $d(d-1)/2$ edges) in the projection to the other mode.

An example of data with more than two modes are the *meta-networks* of Carley (2002). These are collections of one-mode and two-mode networks that result from combinations of several modes. For example, people P, organizations O, and locations L may form PP, PO, PL, OO, OL, and LL networks.

4.2   Indexing and Grouping

Numerous structural indicators have been devised to describe and analyze, for example, the particular structure of a given network, the relative position of actors in it, and the decomposition into meaningful groups of actors.

We will not attempt to enumerate them all. Instead, we will cover the most common methods for the most common analytic tasks in a systematic way. We will also provide pointers to more sophisticated and less frequently used methods, where appropriate. The crucial descriptive tasks addressed in this section are summarized in the following three guiding questions:

– What are the overall characteristics of the network?
– Who are the most influential actors?
– Which actors form meaningful groups in the network?

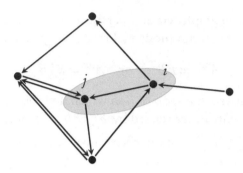

Figure 20: Dyad formed by vertices i and j. While being adjacent, the dyad is not mutual.

What distinguishes network analysis from other, more commonly applied techniques for empirical data analysis is the inherently relational nature of the data. Consequently, an analysis is often based on (possibly derived) relations between actors and the units of analysis are dyads rather than actors.

Hence, we begin this section with indicators that allow the quantification of direct and indirect pair-wise relations of various kinds. While more elaborate indicators are defined in the subsequent sections, in most cases, they only involve the aggregation of the elementary indices presented next.

4.2.1   Dyads as the Unit of Analysis

A dyad is a pair of actors that may or may not be linked by a tie. Dyads are thus represented by pairs of vertices, irrespective of whether these are connected by an edge or not. Dyads are the basic unit of analysis for social networks as other methods are essentially based on the aggregation of dyadic information.

Since most other indicators are derived from dyad indices, the choice of an appropriate dyad index is essential and should be guided by theoretical reasoning about the nature of the relationships between dyad members. For most of the indices discussed below, we will provide examples of instances in which they may be appropriate.

Since a dyad index is supposed to capture the nature of a relation it is closely tied to the type of network under examination. The method of aggregation, on the other hand, determines how positions and compositions are constructed, and is therefore more closely tied to the interest we have in a network.

Elementary Dyad Indices

Simple examples of dyad indices are derived immediately from the presence or absence of edges in a graph $G = (V, E)$. The vertices i, j of a dyad are called *adjacent*, if $(i, j) \in E$ or $(j, i) \in E$, and a dyad is *mutual* or *symmetric*, if $(i, j) \in E$ and $(j, i) \in E$. In terms of elements of the adjacency matrix, these concepts can be expressed equivalently as

$$\text{adjacent:} \quad a_{ij} + a_{ji} > 0$$
$$\text{mutual:} \quad a_{ij} + a_{ji} = 2.$$

Please note that there is no difference between these two conditions in the case of symmetric relations, and that the vertices in a mutual dyad are necessarily adjacent.

Many other quantities can be derived directly from relations between the two actors of a dyad. If data on multiple relations are available, for instance, one can define a *degree of multiplexity* in terms of the number of ties in any of these relations for the same dyad. Likewise, *valued* relations, such as interaction *frequency*, immediately yield a dyad index. An example of a dyad index derived from non-network data is *dissimilarity* based on vertex attributes.

The following are indices that take into account the entire structure, in which a dyad is embedded.

Distance

To define a (structural) concept of distance between two actors, it is necessary to specify how actors can reach each other. Therefore, we define a (directed) *path* in a (directed) graph $G = (V, E)$ as a sequence of edges such that the endpoint of one is the starting point of the next.

Let $s, t \in V$ be any two vertices. Then a sequence of edges (i_0, i_1), $(i_1, i_2), \ldots, (i_{k-1}, i_k) \in E$ with $i_0 = s$ and $i_k = t$ is called a *(directed) st–path*. A sequence of edges that forms an *st*–path after reversing any number of them is called an *undirected st*–path. A path is called *simple*, if no vertex (and thus no edge) is contained twice.

If an *st*–path exists, then t is *reachable* from s. If t is reachable from s and vice versa, then s and t are said to be *(strongly) connected*. They are

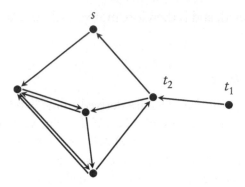

Figure 21: While vertex t_1 is not reachable from s, t_2 has (shortest-path) distance 3 from s. Hence, $d_G(s, t_1) = \infty$ and $d_G(s, t_2) = 3$). The graph is weakly connected but has two strongly connected components, one of which consists only of t_1.

weakly connected, if at least one undirected *st*–path exists, otherwise *s* and *t* are *disconnected*. The inclusion-maximal subgraphs in which all pairs of vertices are strongly or weakly connected are called the strongly or weakly connected *components*. Note that there is no difference between strong and weak connectedness in undirected graphs.

Connectedness and reachability are thus relations (of indirect linkage) derived from the elementary relation of adjacency (i.e., direct linkage), where only connectedness is necessarily symmetric. They can be valued by considering the *length* of paths, i.e., the number of edges in the sequence. Alternatively, if the edge-relation is already valued, the edge values can be aggregated into path values. The most common and intuitive example is a network of locations in which edges are valued by spatial distance. The length of a path is then the sum of the edge lengths, i.e., the total distance along its edges. Graphs without edge values are often treated as a special case of valued graphs, in which all values are uniformly one. In this case, the sum of edge values and the number of edges coincide so that the former is a proper generalization of the latter.

The minimum length of an *st*–path is an essential dyad index, and called (*shortest-path* or *geodesic*) *distance*. It is the lowest number of edges needed to go from *s* to *t*, and denoted by $d_G(s, t)$ or simply $d(s, t)$ if it is clear which graph *G* is referred to. See Figure 21 for an example.

Note that higher-level indices based on shortest-path distances thus embody the assumption that connections between actors are established

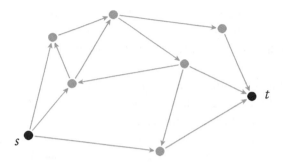

Figure 22: The dyad $\{s, t\}$ *has lower vertex connectivity than edge connectivity,* $v(s, t) = 2 < 3 = \lambda(s, t)$.

along the shortest possible routes. If the relation studied does not grant this assumption, alternative notions of distance may be applicable. For example, the current in an electrical network spreads along paths of any length, but in an energy-efficient way with more current flowing along paths of less resistance. Since this is determined by the resistance in each wire and the way that wires are joined, the effective resistance that needs to be overcome between two network nodes is also a measure of distance derived from aggregated edge values. It appears that current flow is a reasonable model, e.g., for the spreading of rumors.

It is thus crucial to be aware of the implicit assumptions that arise with a particular spreading model. We will return to this issue when discussing centrality indices.

Connectivity

While distances generally evaluate the difficulty actors have in reaching other actors, a *connectivity* index quantifies the ease or certainty of reaching them. If a dyad is connected via two independent paths, this can be interpreted as an indication that reachability is more reliable.

The two most common concepts of connectivity are *vertex connectivity* and *edge connectivity*. A dyad $s, t \in V$ is called *k-vertex-connected*, or simply *k-connected*, if there are at least k st–paths that do not share a vertex other than s and t. Equivalently, at least k vertices must be removed to cut all st–paths. The maximum k for which s and t are k-connected is the *(vertex) connectivity*, $v(s, t)$, of s and t.

If connectivity is not intercepted at vertices but at edges, we are interested in the *edge connectivity*, $\lambda(s,t)$, of s and t. It is defined analoguosly with $s, t \in V$ being *k-edge-connected*, if there are at least k st–paths that do not share an edge. Equivalently, at least k edges must be removed to cut all st–paths.

It is plausible (and can indeed be proven) that $v(s,t) \leq \lambda(s,t)$ for every dyad $s, t \in V$ of every graph $G = (V, E)$. An example in which strict inquality holds is provided in Figure 22.

Connectivity indices are employed, e.g., in applications such as communication network design where tolerance to network failure is important. However, they are also used to define concepts of cohesion, and will hence be revisited in the subsequent section on grouping.

As for distances, there are numerous ways of defining connectivity. The amount of current flowing between two nodes in an electrical network is inversely related to the resistance between them and thus a notion of connectivity. Similarly, there is the concept of network flow, that is not subject to resistance but capacity constraints on the edges.

Embeddedness

The final class of dyad indices considered here does not evaluate the nature of connections between two actors but compares the connections they maintain with others.

In the simplest of all cases, two vertices have exactly the same neighbors (possibly excluding themselves). Since their network positions are indistinguishable, any pair of such vertices is called *structurally equivalent*. Note that this new dyadic relation is reflexive (a vertex always has the same neighbors as itself), symmetric, and transitive (if a vertex has the same neighbors as another, and this second one has the same neighbors as a third vertex, then the first and third necessarily also have the same neighbors), and therefore induces a partition into classes of equivalent vertices. It is thus a method of grouping actors as discussed in Section 4.2.5 below.

An important weaker relation called a *Simmelian tie* is defined for undirected graphs by requiring that the two vertices are adjacent and have at least one neighbor in common (Krackhardt 1999). The resulting relation is a subset of the original relation, restricting adjacencies to pairs of vertices that are members of a triangle.

These non-valued relations can be valued by the *degree of overlap* in neighborhoods, i.e., the commonality of the two sets $N(i)$ and $N(j)$ of neighbors of vertices i and j. Note that in directed graphs, we may

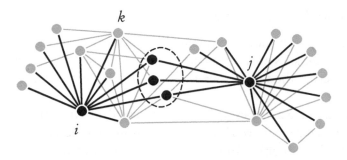

Figure 23: Barely overlapping neighborhoods with Jaccard index $J_G(i,j) = \frac{3}{21} \approx 0.14$ and Euclidean neighborhood distance $\sqrt{18} \approx 4.24$. For comparison, $J_G(i,k) = \frac{7}{13} \approx 0.54$.

also be interested in the overlap of in-neighbors and out-neighbors separately. Multiple measures for quantifying the overlap of any two sets exist (see, e.g., Sneath and Sokal 1973) and can thus be applied to neighborhoods. Two of the more common of these are the number of joint neighbors, $|N(i) \cap N(j)|$, and the relative number of joint neighbors, $J_G(i,j) = \frac{|N(i) \cap N(j)|}{|N(i) \cup N(j)|}$ (known as the *Jaccard index*). These are similarity indices, but since $J_G(i,j)$ is always in the range from 0 to 1, we can construct a *Jaccard distance* from $1 - J_G(i,j)$.

A common measure of dissimilarity that also takes the joint absence of ties into account is the *Euclidean neighborhood distance* of the characteristic vectors of neighborhoods, i.e., the Euclidean distance of the two rows or columns in the adjacency matrix. For out-neighborhoods, the Euclidean neighborhood distance is the Euclidean distance of the row vectors A_i and A_j in the adjacency matrix A,

$$\|A_i - A_j\| = \sqrt{\sum_{k \in V} (a_{ik} - a_{jk})^2} \, .$$

Similar concepts of this kind include *Hamming distance* (counting the number of vertices that are adjacent to one of i and j but not the other) and *neighborhood correlation* (correlation of the row or column vectors of the adjacency matrix).

4.2.2   Network Characteristics

Before dealing with more fine-grained indicators, let us consider some coarse characteristics of an entire network. These are intended to be helpful in answering the first of our three guiding questions mentioned on p. 111.

Network characteristics are especially useful in comparative studies when the variance in network structure is assumed to be a cause or consequence of other variables. In fact, this is the main hypothesis underlying ego network analysis, in which characteristics of personal networks are used as features of individuals (i.e., of the egos). Please note that it may be easier to survey the characteristics directly than to collect the actual network first and then determine the quantity of interest from it.

Density

The simplest such indicator is a network's *density*, which is defined as the ratio of the number of edges to the number of dyads, i.e., the ratio of the number of actual to possible edges. While the number of dyads $D(G) = \{\{i,j\} : i \neq j \in V\}$ in a graph is always $\frac{n(n-1)}{2}$, the number of edges a dyad can have depends on whether the graph is directed or undirected. We define

$$density(G) = \frac{\text{number of edges}}{\text{number of possible edges in a dyad} \times \text{number of dyads}}$$

and thus obtain $density(G) = \frac{m}{2|D(G)|} = \frac{m}{n(n-1)}$ if G is a directed graph, and $density(G) = \frac{m}{|D(G)|} = \frac{2m}{n(n-1)}$ if it is undirected.

It is instructive to view density from another angle too. Since each edge represents an adjacency, density can be understood as the network average of the dyad-level adjacency index.

Although intuitive as a measure, density has an undesirable scaling behavior. Assume that the network data were collected via questionnaries using a limited-choice design, i.e., each respondent was allowed to name at most k alteri, where k is a constant, say $k = 5$. For simplicity, let us assume that every respondent named exactly k alteri, and that all alteri are also respondents. If the resulting network has n vertices (respondents), it has $k \cdot n$ directed edges (nominations). Its density is therefore $\frac{kn}{n(n-1)} = \frac{k}{n-1}$. Since k is constant, density is tending to zero by design with increasing sample size n.

This vanishing behavior is encountered quite generally as, even in free-choice questionnaire designs, the average number of nominations is usually bounded by a constant so that the total number of nominations behaves as in the above example.

For an alternative, observe that the average outdegree is at most k by design in the above example. The deviation from k is hence a reasonable indicator of how many nominations were made in comparison to how many were allowed. Since the total outdegree always equals the number of edges, the average outdegree equals density times $n - 1$. For networks that are typically sparse, the average degree is generally a better measure of whether the number of edges is large or small, and therefore preferred to density.

In the same way that density summarizes adjacency, *reciprocity* summarizes mutuality. It is expressed as a fraction of the adjacent dyads,

$$reciprocity(G) = \frac{\text{number of mutual dyads}}{\text{number of adjacent dyads}},$$

because counting in all non-adjacent dyads also results in an over-emphasis if these are considered as mutual and an under-emphasis if they are considered as non-mutual (compliant with the above definition of mutuality).

Degrees

A frequently used network characteristic is the distribution of degrees, i.e., the fractions of vertices having the same degree. Note that degree is itself a vertex-level aggregation of a dyad index, namely the number of adjacent dyads, in which a vertex is involved. It should also be recalled that we defined a variant concept of density by averaging over all vertex degrees.

Many graphs representing observed networks have been found to contain vertices of surprisingly high degree. More precisely, their *degree sequences* display a scaling behavior defined as follows. Let $d_1 \geq d_2 \geq \ldots \geq d_n$ be the size-ordered sequence of degrees in an undirected graph, then this sequence is said to (approximately) satisfy a *power law* with exponent α, if

$$i \approx c \cdot d_i^{-\alpha}$$

for any constant c and all $i = 1, \ldots, n$. The scatterplot with points (d_i, i) is called *size-rank* plot, and taking the logarithm on both axes yields points lying close to a line with slope $-\alpha$.

Graphs with a power-law degree sequence are called *scale free* for the following reason. Let us assume we are observing a different graph G' with n' vertices satisfying a power law with the same parameters c, α. This can be interpreted as changing the resolution on the y-axis of the size-rank plot; depending on whether n' is larger or smaller than n we add or remove points. Now fix a rank $1 \leq i \leq n$ and consider a corresponding rank $1 \leq i' \leq n'$ that is in approximately the same position after the resolution has been changed, i.e. $\frac{i'}{i} \approx \frac{n'}{n}$. Since the degree sequence $d'_1 \geq \ldots \geq d'_{n'}$ of G' satisfies $i' \approx c \cdot (d'_{i'})^{-\alpha}$ for all $i' = 1, \ldots, n'$, it follows that $\frac{n'}{n} \approx \frac{i'}{i} \approx \left(\frac{d'_{i'}}{d_i} \right)^{-\alpha}$ and therefore $\frac{d'_{i'}}{d_i} \approx \left(\frac{n'}{n} \right)^{-\frac{1}{\alpha}}$, so that the x-axis is essentially scaled by a constant as well. Hence, scaling the size of the graph only results in a corresponding scaling of degrees. For more details on this, see Cooper and Lu (2007).

Please note that if a degree sequence scales with exponent α, degree frequencies also scale with exponent $\gamma = 1 + \alpha$. The interpretation of frequencies as probabilities leads to the graphic interpretation that high-degree vertices are much more likely than they would be in a normal distribution. However, it is a common mistake to start from the seemingly more intuitive frequencies and infer a scaling behavior by fitting lines in doubly logarithmic size-frequency plots (Li, Alderson, Doyle, and Willinger 2005).

Connectivity

The notion of dyad connectivity discussed above can be extended to the entire network. We say that an undirected graph is *connected*, if each dyad is connected. If it is not connected, the inclusion-maximal subsets of vertices that are pair-wise connected are called the *connected components*.

Most commonly, dyad connectivity is extended to entire graphs not by averaging but by taking the minimum. For communication and infrastructure networks, the minimum edge or vertex connectivity between any pair of vertices in the corresponding graph is an indicator of the fault tolerance or attack resilience of the network.

The (weakly) connected components of a graph can often be treated separately because there are no ties creating dependencies between them. Some network-analytic measures require that a graph is connected, or strongly connected, to be well-defined. It may, therefore, be necessary to check for connectivity prior to carrying out an analysis.

Distance

A simple network characteristic based on distances is *Wiener's Index*, $W(G) = \sum_{s,t \in V} d_G(s,t)$ (Wiener 1947), where $d_G(s,t)$ is the shortest-path distance from s to t. It is a requirement that the graph be strongly connected since the index is infinite or undefined if there is a dyad with vertices that are not mutually reachable. Please remember that $d_G(s,t) = 0$ if $s = t$ and observe that each dyad is counted twice (once in each direction). To avoid double counting in undirected graphs, the above value can be divided by two.

The normalized version of Wiener's Index representing the average distance of each pair is referred to as the *characteristic path length*, $L(G) = \frac{1}{n(n-1)} W(G)$ and one of the criteria used to classify networks as *small worlds* (Watts and Strogatz 1998).

Configuration Counts

As in many variations of the above examples and other dyad-level or vertex-level indices, network characteristics can be obtained from their distribution and statistics of these distributions.

A different class of network characteristics is obtained from counting configurations rather than aggregating lower-level indices. A simple example is the *dyad census* of a directed graph. Since vertices of any dyad can be linked by at most two edges, it consists of three values for the number of mutual, asymmetric, and null dyads (Holland and Leinhardt 1970).

The next biggest example is the *triad census* (Holland and Leinhardt 1976), in which the frequency of all 16 possible configurations of the three dyads formed by three vertices as shown in Figure 24 are determined. More generally, one is often interested in particular, or particularly frequent, subgraphs which are then referred to as *motifs*. Counting statistics are pivotal in network modeling as discussed in Section 4.3.

Macro Shapes

Some aggregates of lower-level indices serve to characterize certain tendencies that relate to images of a global shape of the network. As one dimension of informal organization, Krackhardt (1994) quantifies the degree to which a graph is *hierarchic* as $1 - reciprocity(G_r)$, where G_r is the graph defined by the reachability relation and *reciprocity* is as defined on p. 119. A relation such as pecking is thus hierarchic, if the number of

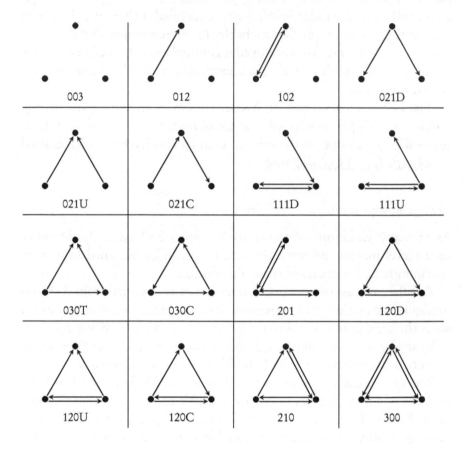

Figure 24: Triad types in directed networks. The conventional numbering scheme is based on the number of mutual, asymmetric, and null dyads (MAN for short), with trailing characters U: up, D: down, T: transitive, and C: cyclic.

dyads in which one actor can reach the other but not vice versa is relatively high (see also Everett and Krackhardt 2012).

A summary statistic of vertex-level indices is *centralization* (Freeman 1979). A vertex centrality assigns values to vertices that quantify the structural importance of vertices, and we treat them extensively below. One such index is simply the degree of a vertex. Whether a graph is centralized is then assessed by the degree to which few vertices are notably more central than the others,

$$\frac{\sum_{i \in V} \hat{c} - c(i)}{C(n)},$$

where $c(i)$ is the centrality of vertex $i \in V$, $\hat{c} = \max_{j \in V} c(j)$ is highest centrality of any vertex in the graph, and $C(n)$ is the maximum value that the numerator can attain in any graph with the same number n of vertices.

Centralization is superficially related to the concept of having a *core-periphery structure*. The latter refers to the possibility of classifying the actors into a cohesive core and a non-cohesive periphery (Borgatti and Everett 1999). Core-periphery structures can also occur as artifacts of poor boundary specification or snowball sampling.

4.2.3 Centrality

We shall now address the second guiding question of this section by introducing methods developed for the identification of (structurally) important actors and, more generally, the relative importance of all actors. In fact, this is one of the primary tasks in network analysis.

The most common approach to this task is the assignment of values to actors such that larger values correspond to greater importance. In this scenario, centrality is an actor-level index, and we will present several indices that, together, can be considered representative.

Most actor-level indices are aggregates of dyad-level indices from precisely those dyads in which the actor is involved. The most elementary ones are *degrees* and can be considered as measures of an actor's activity or involvement. These are simple counts of the number of adjacencies of the corresponding vertex. We define

$$\text{indegree} \quad d^-(i) = \sum_{j \in V} a_{ji}$$
$$\text{outdegree} \quad d^+(i) = \sum_{j \in V} a_{ij}$$
$$\text{degree} \quad d(i) = d^-(i) + d^+(i)$$

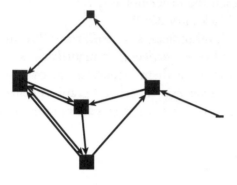

node area:	total degree
node width:	outdegree
node height:	indegree

Figure 25: Degree visualized in terms of node size.

While, say, indegree corresponds to the number of in-neighbors in non-valued graphs, the above definition generalizes to valued and multigraphs. In undirected graphs, in-neighbors and out-neighbors are the same and degree is therefore defined as $d(i) = d^-(i) = d^+(i)$.

Obviously, we can define similar actor indices by replacing adjacencies with any other dyad-level index such as mutuality.

Centralities are probably the most commonly used actor-level indices. There is no agreement as to what exactly centrality is and which properties a centrality index should satisfy (Freeman 1979) but, in general, the idea is that centralities express a structural advantage, importance, or dominance.

In this sense, degree is a centrality index because activity may already be an indication of importance. The oldest example of this kind is *sociometric choice*, in which the popularity of an actor is operationalized as the indegree of the corresponding vertex.

Radial Centralities

A more elaborate way of defining an actor centrality is, again, to aggregate information over all dyads involving the actor of interest. An example of this is *closeness centrality* (Bavelas 1950; Sabidussi 1966),

$$c_C(i) = \frac{1}{\sum_{t \in V} d(i,t)} = \frac{1}{\text{total distance to all other vertices}} \,,$$

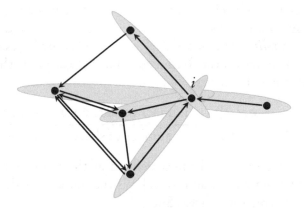

Figure 26: Radial dyads centered on i.

in which the inverse of the sum of distances to all other vertices is taken so that large distances correspond to low centralities. Closeness is thus an example of what is termed a *radial* notion of centrality because the underlying principle is that the centrality of an actor is defined in terms of the dyadic relations of this actor with everyone else in the network (Borgatti and Everett 2006). Obviously, the dyadic relation may be instantiated with any of the dyad indices discussed above (distance, connectivity, etc.), and we can also aggregate them in various ways (sum, harmonic sum, maximum, median, etc.).

The choice of dyad index should be guided by the kind of network relation considered (Borgatti 2005). When studying a network of personal communication links, for example, the importance of an actor as a source of rumors may be defined using a dyad-level index that models how likely it is that a rumor originating from one actor will arrive at the other within a given time span and without alteration. The aggregation of these indices with the same source vertex then evaluates its overall importance for placing rumors.

Burt (1992) also defines a radial centrality, *constraint*, by summing redundancy (as defined on p. 131) over all dyads, in which the actor participates.

Medial Centralities

Instead of assessing the position of an actor by aggregating over all dyads, in which the actor is involved, we can aggregate over all other dyads the importance of the actor's position for that dyad.

One interpretation of such involvement is the dependency of a dyad on the actor of interest to serve as an intermediary. The standard example is *betweenness centrality* (Freeman 1977). Each dyad contributes the dependency of its members on the focal actor. For betweenness, this is called *pair-dependency* and defined as

$$\delta(s,t|i) = \frac{\sigma(s,t|i)}{\sigma(s,t)} = \frac{\text{number of shortest } st\text{–paths via } i}{\text{number of shortest } st\text{–paths}}$$

where $\sigma(s,t)$ is a dyad-level index defined as the number of different shortest paths from s to t, and $\sigma(s,t|i)$ is the number of those that involve i as an intermediate vertex. Since

$$\sigma(s,t|i) = \begin{cases} \sigma(s,i) \cdot \sigma(i,t) & \text{if } d_G(s,t) = d_G(s,i) + d_G(i,t) \\ 0 & \text{otherwise}, \end{cases}$$

$\sigma(s,t|i)$ and also $\delta(s,t|i)$ are easily recognized as a dyad index derived from another one (shortest-path distance). Betweenness centrality is obtained by aggregating dependencies over all dyads that do not contain the focal actor,

$$c_B(i) = \sum_{s \neq i \neq t \in V} \delta(s,t|i).$$

Again, pair-dependency based on shortest paths can be replaced by dependencies based on other dyad-level indices, such as current flow or connectivity, and selecting the appropriate one is a substantive matter.

Feedback Centralities

Feedback refers to the dependence of an actor's centrality on the centrality of other actors. The classic example of this kind is *eigenvector centrality* (Bonacich 1972; 1987; Bonacich and Lloyd 2001), which is defined by

$$c_E(i) = \alpha \sum_{j \in N^-(i)} c_E(j)$$

where $\lambda = \frac{1}{\alpha}$ is an eigenvalue of the adjacency matrix. Please note that the resulting system of linear equations has one equation per vertex and it can be written as $Ac_E = \lambda c_E$, where A is the adjacency matrix of the graph. If the graph is undirected or strongly connected, and λ is selected as the largest eigenvalue of A, this system has a unique solution with only positive entries. Note that we can replace the in-neighbors by any other neighborhood.

The rationale underlying eigenvector centrality is straightforward. An actor's centrality is proportional to the total centrality of its neighbors. Conversely, an actor contributes its own centrality to each of its neighbors. This implies that the contribution must be understood as something replicable that scales to any number of neighbors. If the contributions that can be made are limited, for example because it requires time to pass on importance, it may be better to divide the contribution by the number of recipients as in

$$c(i) = \alpha \sum_{j \in N^-(i)} \frac{c_e(j)}{d^+(j)} \, .$$

Interestingly, in undirected graphs this yields $\alpha = 1$ and is equivalent to degree. In directed graphs it is more informative but requires strong connectivity. A variant that circumvents this problem is the *PageRank index* used in Google's search engine (Brin and Page 1998),

$$c_P(i) = (1 - \omega) \left(\sum_{j \in N^-(i)} \frac{c_P(j)}{d^+(j)} \right) + \omega \frac{1}{n(G)} \, ,$$

where the second term corresponds to artifical links that fully connect the graph but have low and uniform weight, and $0 < \omega < 1$ is a parameter trading off structure versus the uniform a-priori influence.

Interestingly, feedback centralities can also be expressed in terms of dyad-level indices, although the relation is intricate. For instance, a frequently used measure called *status* (Katz 1953) can be defined either in feedback terms as

$$c_S(i) = \sum_{(j,i) \in V} \alpha \cdot (1 + c_S(j))$$

where $0 < \alpha < 1$ is a sufficiently small constant, or as a radial centrality based on the sum over dyad scores

$$c_S(i) = \sum_{s \in V} \chi_\alpha(s, i)$$

where $\chi_\alpha(s, i)$ is the sum over all (simple or not) si–paths of any length, where the contribution of paths of length k is weighted by α^k, i.e., longer walks contribute less. This dyad index thus considers direct and indirect choices, and therefore generalizes sociometric choice.

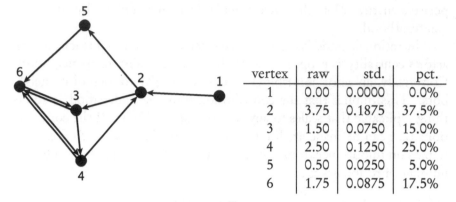

vertex	raw	std.	pct.
1	0.00	0.0000	0.0%
2	3.75	0.1875	37.5%
3	1.50	0.0750	15.0%
4	2.50	0.1250	25.0%
5	0.50	0.0250	5.0%
6	1.75	0.0875	17.5%

Figure 27: Betweenness centrality scores: raw values, standardized by dividing by the maximum possible score of $5 \cdot 4 = 20$, and normalized by their sum 10. Relative scores remain the same within the network, but need not across networks.

Choosing a Centrality Index

The relations between radial, medial, and feedback centralities are not fully understood. Nevertheless, reasonably educated choices can be made by considering the following two dimensions.

Dyad index: In your study, you will investigate particular kinds of ties, and have specific theories and ideas about how actors relate directly or indirectly through these ties. Identifying a dyad-level index that reflects the nature of these relations is, therefore, the crucial first step.

Aggregation: In a second step, the way, in which these relations yield special positions, is derived from theories of, e.g., power attribution, and operationalized in (i) the choice of dyads and (ii) the way their evaluations are aggregated.

Comparing Actor Centralities

Centrality scores are usually considered as being ordinal, i.e., while the rank of an actor's score in the sorted list of all scores is important, the absolute value is not. To compare actor centrality across networks, however, scores must be mapped to a common scale. Two main approaches have been proposed and whereas in both cases scores are mapped to lie in the interval from zero to one, the reference quantity is different.

Standardization: Each vertex centrality score is divided by the maximum possible score for a vertex in any graph with the same number of vertices (Freeman 1979). Therefore, the standardized score is one exactly when a vertex cannot be more central in any configuration with the same number of others. Usually, but not always, this corresponds to comparing the position of a vertex with that of the center of a star.
The advantage is that the centrality of an actor is assessed in absolute terms, compared to what is possible. A disadvantage is that this theoretical maximum is not always well-defined (as is the case with eigenvector centrality, for instance) and that it is difficult to compare the centrality of actors in networks of different sizes. Even for networks with the same number of vertices, it could be argued that the maximum should really be determined only among graphs that also have the same number of edges.

Normalization: Instead of an absolute benchmark, you can use the scores of the other vertices in the graph for reference. This is achieved by dividing each centrality score by the sum of all scores, which yields the share of importance that a vertex received. Such a relative notion enables comparison across all kinds of networks, and even centrality measures. However, it is not possible to state that a score is high or low in absolute terms.

Neither transformation changes the rank order of actors in the same network. Since standardization is proposed in Freeman (1979), it is the default form for presenting centrality scores in many tools for network analysis, although sum-normalized scores are more generally applicable. We already pointed out at the end of Section 4.2.2 that summary statistics of the centrality distribution can be used to characterize the network as a whole.

Edge Centralities

In this section, we briefly discuss means of assessing the importance of individual edges. This is very similar to what we have just discussed for vertices.

In fact, concepts introduced for vertices carry over to edges as we can transform a graph into a new graph that has a vertex for every edge of the original one, and two of these new vertices are adjacent, if the original edges share a vertex. More precisely, a directed graph $G = (V, E)$ yields a *line graph* $\mathscr{L}(G) = (E, \{(e_1, e_2) : e_1 = (i, j), e_2 = (j, k) \in E\})$. Line graphs thus reflect how edges are connected among themselves, and any vertex index can be applied to the line graph to define an edge index in the original graph.

However, genuine edge indices also exist. In his seminal paper, Granovetter (1973) distinguishes strong and weak ties based on a forbidden triad configuration. As this classification is not unique, however, he also proposes a valued assessment of the importance of an edge for shortcutting otherwise distant dyads. An edge (i,j) of a non-valued graph G is called a k-*bridge*, if $d_{G-(i,j)}(i,j) \geq k$, i.e., if the distance from i to j is at least k if (i,j) is removed. Edges that are k-bridges for some large k are considered indicative of weak ties because they link distant vertices.

A similar operationalization of weak ties is based on betweenness. A proper extension of the pair-dependencies on intermediate vertices defined above is

$$\delta(s,t|(i,j)) = \begin{cases} \sigma(s,i)\cdot\sigma(j,t) & \text{if } d(s,t)=d(s,i)+1+d(j,t) \\ 0 & \text{otherwise,} \end{cases}$$

so that an *edge betweenness centrality* can be defined as

$$c_B(e) = \sum_{s,t\in V} \frac{\sigma(s,t|e)}{\sigma(s,t)}.$$

Since, unfortunately, this index does not coincide with vertex betweenness centrality in the line graph, care must be taken in choosing an appropriate index.

4.2.4   Cohesion

Cohesion denotes the tendency towards dense, redundant connections. For example, we may want to assess the cohesion of a team because a group performance theory relates it with effectiveness. More generally, the variance in cohesion across a network can be used to identify cohesive groups and thus provide one type of answer to the third guiding question of this section.

We have already discussed an elementary index for cohesion, namely (network-level) density. Since density is defined as the ratio of existing to possible edges, it can be defined for any subnetwork by restricting the set of dyads taken into consideration. Some actor-level and group-level versions of density are listed below for comparison with more sophisticated methods.

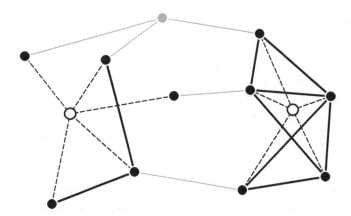

Figure 28: Two neighborhoods of size 5 with different density. The left one has density $\frac{2}{5 \cdot 4} = 0.1$, the right one $\frac{7}{20} = 0.35$. By definition, these values are the clustering coefficients of the two vertices defining these neighborhoods.

Actor Level

On the actor level, cohesion refers to the tight integration of an actor into the surrounding structure. The best-known measure of cohesion on the actor level is the *clustering coefficient* (Watts and Strogatz 1998), which is simply the density of the graph induced by the neighborhood of an actor. Whereas degree is defined in terms of the number of neighbors, the clustering coefficient is based on their interconnectedness.

We have already argued, however, that density has undesirable scaling properties, and thus recommended that average degree be used instead. In fact, Burt (1992) defines the *redundancy* in an actor's neighborhood as the average degree of its members in the induced subgraph.[1] In addition to redundancy, Burt (1992) defines three other cohesion-based indicators describing the neighborhood of an actors.

The opposite of cohesion among neighbors is their segregation. In particular, an actor may be a *broker* that is vital for dyad-level indices of connectivity in the sense that these deteriorate when its vertex is removed from the graph. In the extreme case, the graph is no longer connected without this vertex.

---

1 This is actually a simplified interpretation of redundancy in unweighted graphs pointed out in Borgatti (1997).

Group Level

A cohesive group is a group of actors with higher internal than external cohesion. The most cohesive group imaginable is one in which all members are pair-wise adjacent. A set $C \subseteq V$ of vertices in a graph is called a *clique* (Luce and Perry 1949), if all dyads in the induced graph $G[C]$ are mutual. Remember that mutual and adjacent are the same in undirected graphs and note that any subset of a clique also forms a clique. A common form of analysis is, therefore, the enumeration of all inclusion-maximal cliques of at least three vertices.

In observed networks, there may be few inclusion-maximal cliques and their size is usually small. This is because the requirement for a set of vertices to form a clique is extreme, and a single missing edge rules out the enlargement of a clique. Of the many weaker concepts of strong internal cohesion of a group, we mention just one, k-cores.

The k-*core* of an undirected graph is a vertex-induced subgraph $G[C_k]$ induced by an inclusion-maximal set of vertices $C_k \subseteq V$ such that every vertex $i \in C_k$ has at least k neighbors in C_k, i.e., the induced degree $d_{G[C_k]}(i) \geq k$ (Seidman 1983). Note that C_k may be smaller than the set of all vertices of degree at least k in the whole graph G. In fact, the k-core of a graph is uniquely defined for all $k = 0, \ldots, n - 1$. Since cores are nested, i.e., the $k + 1$-core is a subgraph of the k-core, we have a successively stronger requirement.

On the other hand, the following example shows that by focussing on degree, we may lose the connectivity aspect of cohesion. Consider a graph consisting of two separate cliques of $k + 1$ vertices each. These two cliques together then form the k-core because each vertex has, indeed, at least k neighbors in this graph.

If connectivity is more important than degree, a corresponding concept of group cohesion can also be defined. A λ-*set* is a subset of vertices $C \subseteq V$, in which every internal dyad has a higher edge-connectivity than any dyad that involves a member and a non-member of that group (Borgatti, Everett, and Shirey 1990). Again, we obtain a nested structure of successively more cohesive groups.

Despite the differences between them, all of the above concepts share the property that each subset of vertices is either a group in the corresponding sense or not. This is because cohesion is defined as an absolute requirement and, consequently, a graph may not contain any cohesive group.

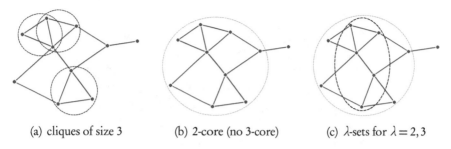

<table>
<tr><td>(a) cliques of size 3</td><td>(b) 2-core (no 3-core)</td><td>(c) λ-sets for $\lambda = 2, 3$</td></tr>
</table>

Figure 29: Comparison of cliques, cores, and λ-sets.

Clustering

Without an absolute definition of cohesion, a graph can nevertheless be decomposed into relatively cohesive groups by trading-off internal cohesion against external separation. The strategy is to determine a set $\mathscr{C} = \{C_1, \ldots, C_r\}$ of *clusters*. Commonly, $\mathscr{C}$ is a *partition*, i.e., the clusters are disjoint, non-empty, and cover the set of vertices. Overlapping clusters are sometimes also considered, however.

Various objective functions have been proposed for assessing the quality of a partition with respect to the internal-external criterion (Schaeffer 2007; Fortunato 2010). The one currently used most frequently is called *modularity* and defined as

$$Q(\mathscr{C}) = \sum_{C \in \mathscr{C}} \frac{|m(C)|}{m} - \frac{\sum_{i \in C} d(i)^2}{(2m)^2},$$

where $m(C)$ is the number of edges with both vertices in C (Newman and Girvan 2004).

Modularity thus trades off two competing goals. The first term corresponds to the percentage of edges internal to the clusters and is, therefore, large if clusters are growing. It is maximum for a single cluster covering all edges. For the second term, observe first that the sum over all vertex degrees is twice the number of edges and that the square of a sum of positive values is never smaller than the sum of the squares of these values. The second term is thus small, if vertex degrees are scattered across clusters. It is minimum for the partition, in which every vertex forms a singleton cluster. A partition is thus considered a good clustering, if most edges are internal to clusters but clusters are small and balanced in the total degree of their vertices. An example is given in Figure 30.

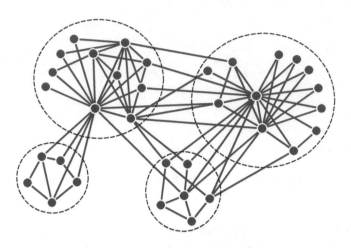

Figure 30: Partition with maximum modularity.

In recent years, extensive research has also unveiled quite a few disadvantages of the modularity objective. Like most other graph clustering methods, it is computationally intractable to optimize (Brandes, Delling, Gaertler, Görke, Hoefer, Nikoloski, and Wagner 2008), and partitions of similarly good quality can be very different (Good, de Montjoye, and Clauset 2010).

On the other hand, if there is a prominent clustering with a high variance of local density, any of the established methods will recover the corresponding partition. The precise relations with network formation theories and difference in outcome are even less well understood than for centrality indices. Hence, for now, at least, you need not worry too much about which graph clustering method to use. It is more important to be careful in the interpretation of results which are bound to be subject to artifacts or arbitrariness.

4.2.5   Roles

Cohesion appears to be a straightforward concept for grouping. Groups need not, however, be characterized by tighter intergration, actors can also be classified by similarity of relations to other (groups of) actors. Just like cohesion, this concept may be defined in various ways.

Nadel (1957), for instance, argued that the relations among actors in a social network are governed by their *roles*, where a role may be defined,

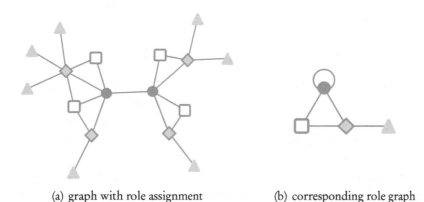

(a) graph with role assignment   (b) corresponding role graph

Figure 31: In a regular role assignment, every pair of vertices having the same role is adjacent to the same other roles.

e.g., by social category, membership in a social group, or other actor characteristics.

Formally, a *role assignment* is a mapping $r : V \rightarrow R$ of vertices $v \in V$ to roles $r(v) \in R$. A role assignment reduces the complexity of a network by abstracting from the individual actors. Think of a food web, in which not individual animals and plants, but their types are represented. The predator-prey relationship of an animal of one type towards one of another type is generally the same for all members of these types (see, e.g., Luczkovich, Borgatti, Johnson, and Everett 2003).

Figure 31 shows how a role assignment can be used to reduce a graph to the corresponding *role graph*. Note that the edges in the role graph only make sense, if they are *compatible* with those in the original graph. Therefore, not every mapping of vertices to roles is a meaningful role assignment. In the following, we will discuss the two main classes of constraints that are used to ensure compatibility of a role assignment with the given structure.

Structural Equivalence

A straightforward and purely structural definition of role, which may or may not have a deeper foundation, is *structural equivalence* (Lorrain and White 1971). Two actors are considered structurally equivalent, only if they have exactly the same neighbors. Thus, structurally equivalent actors can not be distinguished by their relations to others.

A role assignment is based on structural equivalence, if assuming the same role implies having the same neighbors,

$$r(i) = r(j) \quad \Longrightarrow \quad N(i) = N(j).$$

A graph may admit several role assignments based on structural equivalence, some of which are refinements of others. In particular, assigning a different role to each vertex is always compatible with the definition of structural equivalence; this is because no two vertices have the same role, therefore the set of conditions is empty.

On the other hand, structural equivalence is a rather strict concept. A single added or omitted tie may render an otherwise meaningful role assignment infeasible. Relaxations of the concept have been proposed, therefore, in which actors are grouped not by equality but similarity of their neighborhoods. We have already discussed corresponding dyad indices at the end of Section 4.2.1, and in particular the Jaccard coefficient. Groups can be formed from such pair-wise similarities or dissimilarities by applying general data clustering methods. An unconventional approach to classification based on iterated neighborhood correlation is proposed in Breiger, Boorman, and Arabie (1975).

Regular Equivalence

Structural equivalences and their relaxations are inappropriate if the notion of role we are intersted in is not defined in terms of ties with the same actors. Two whales do not play the same role in a food web because they feed on the same krill but because they both feed on krill.

The prototypical example in which roles are defined in terms of relations to actors who are not necessarily the same but have the same role, is called *regular equivalence* (White and Reitz 1983). A role assignment based on regular equivalence must satisfy

$$r(i) = r(j) \quad \Longrightarrow \quad r(N(i)) = r(N(j))$$

where $r(N(i))$ is the set of roles in the neighborhood of $i \in V$. Note that this introduces a notion of feedback into the definition, similar to what we did with centralities. Note also that the number of occurrences of a role in a neighborhood does not matter. The roles in Figure 31 are indeed based on regular equivalence, and the two diamond-shaped vertices on the left have a different number of triangle-shaped neighbors. If we require that the number of neighbors having the same role also be equal, i.e., if we interpret $r(N(i))$ as a multiset, the role assignment is said to be based on *exact equivalence* (Everett and Borgatti 1996).

Like structural equivalence, regular equivalence may allow for several different role assignments. Again, the trivial role assignment of one role per vertex is compatible with the definition, and, moreover, the assignment of the same role to all vertices does not violate any constraint either, unless there are both isolate and non-isolate vertices. In the majority of cases, we are interested, therefore, in the coarsest role assignment based on regular equivalence that refines a given partition based on other criteria. A number of results about role equivalence relations is compiled in Everett and Borgatti (1994).

4.2.6 Blockmodeling

The general problem of partitioning the actors of a network into groups such that the relations within and between groups are close to some idealized pattern is called *blockmodeling*. The name stems from the adjacency matrix representation, in which rows and columns can be reordered to have groups form intervals. The relationships within groups then appear as quadratic submatrices along the diagonal, and relationships between groups as rectangular off-diagonal submatrices. Both types of submatrices are referred to as *blocks*. A partition is considered feasible, if specific requirements are met by each block.

As initial examples for such requirements, note that the above approaches to clustering and role equivalence are special cases of blockmodeling. In clustering, we seek to determine a partition, in which the diagonal blocks are as full as possible and the non-diagonal blocks as empty as possible. Each of the clustering approaches mentioned has its own specific concept of full and empty. Vertex equivalences, on the other hand, yield blocks that correspond to the defining equivalence relation. Regular equivalence, for instance, yields blocks that are either empty or have at least one non-zero entry in each row and column. These so-called regular blocks indicate that each member of the row group is adjacent to at least one member of the column group.

Similar to the role graph for equivalence classes, we can generate a more abstract view of a blockmodel by replacing each block with a single entry indicating its type as shown in Figure 32. This simplification is called the *image matrix* of a blockmodel.

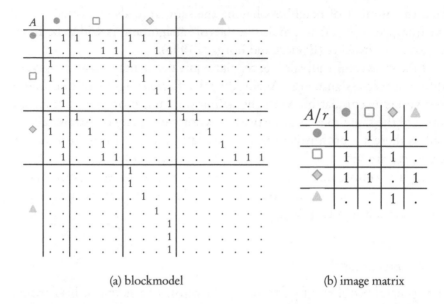

     (a) blockmodel   (b) image matrix

Figure 32: Blockmodel with groups corresponding to the regular equivalence classes of Figure 31. Consequently, all non-empty blocks are regular because they contain at least one 1 in every row and column.

It need not be the case, however, that groups are uniform in the sense that their internal and external relations follow the same pattern across all groups. A simple, yet important, example is given in Figure 33. The image matrix represents a prototypical *core-periphery structure*, in which there is a cohesive center with a periphery of near-isolates.

Several degrees of freedom can be leveraged to fit blockmodels to empirical data (see, e.g., Snijders and Nowicki 1997). Depending on the context, the presence of several groups with special inter-group relations may be anticipated. This corresponds to assuming the presence of certain types of blocks, while others, for which no expectations are made, can be of any type. Moreover, the evaluation of a blockmodel is highly dependent on the way in which the degree of non-conformance with an ideal block type is measured.

To illustrate this point, consider the ideal block types for cohesion-based clustering, namely full and empty blocks. These are almost never observed empirically because they would correspond to a collection of cliques. The relaxations proposed differ in their goodness-of-fit criteria

	core	periphery
core	1	1
periphery	1	0

(a) pre-specified core-periphery image matrix

	core					periphery														
SSR	1	1	1	1	1	.	.	1	.	.	.	1	.	.	.	1	1	1	.	1
CYSR	1	1	.	1	1	1	.	.	1	.	.	.	1	1	1	.	.	.	.	1
JSWE	1	.	1	1	1	.	.	.	.	.	1	1	.	.	1	.	1	1	1	
SCW	1	1	1	1	1	1	.	1	1	.	1	1	.	.	1	1	.	1	1	1
SW	1	1	1	1	1	1	1	1	1	1	1	1	1	1	.	1	.	1	1	1
CAN	.	1	.	1	1	1	.	.	.	.	.	.	1	.	1	.	.	.	.	
AMH	.	.	.	.	1	.	1	.	.	.	.	.	.	.	.	.	.	.	.	
CSWJ	1	.	.	1	1	.	.	1	.	.	.	.	.	.	.	.	.	.	.	
FR	.	1	.	1	1	.	.	.	1	.	.	.	.	.	.	.	.	.	.	
IJSW	.	.	.	.	1	.	.	.	.	1	.	.	.	.	.	.	.	.	.	
JGSW	.	.	.	1	1	.	.	.	.	.	1	.	.	.	.	.	.	.	.	
ASW	1	.	1	1	1	.	.	.	.	.	.	1	.	1	.	.	.	.	.	1
BJSW	.	.	1	.	1	.	.	.	.	.	.	.	1	.	.	.	1	.	.	
PW	.	1	.	.	1	1	.	.	.	.	.	1	.	1	.	1	.	.	.	
CCQ	.	1	.	1	.	.	.	.	.	.	.	.	1	1	.	.	.	.	.	
CW	1	1	1	1	1	1	.	.	.	.	.	1	1	1	.	.	.	.	1	
JSP	1	.	.	.	.	.	.	.	.	.	.	.	.	.	.	1	.	.	.	
SWG	1	.	1	1	1	.	.	.	.	.	.	1	.	.	.	.	1	1	.	
SWHC	.	.	1	1	1	.	.	.	.	.	.	.	.	.	.	.	1	1	.	
SWRA	1	1	1	1	1	.	.	.	.	.	1	.	.	.	1	.	.	.	1	

(b) network fitted to core-periphery model

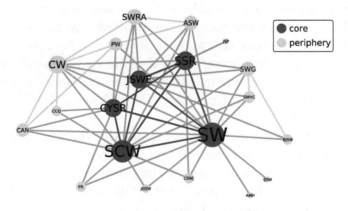

(c) network diagram (size represents degree)

Figure 33: Example of Borgatti and Everett (1999), in which citation data between social work journals (Baker 1992) is fitted to a core-periphery model.

and, in many cases, these can be separated into goodness-of-fit statistics for the individual blocks.

Almost all criteria other than role equivalence lead to computationally intractable partitioning problems. Hence, the software tools available for blockmodeling resort to heuristic algorithms which generally yield suboptimal solutions. Interpretation should therefore be careful and generally avoid focusing on individuals. A comprehensive overview of block types, fitting methods, and interpretation of blockmodels is provided in Doreian, Batagelj, and Ferligoj (2005).

4.3   Modeling

Models express our – often simplified – assumptions about underlying mechanisms or possible outcomes. Statistical models, in particular, express our assumptions about associations between variables that are subject to noise, measurement error, or uncertainty.

Goldenberg, Zheng, Fienberg, and Airoldi (2009) and Snijders (2011) provide detailed and comprehensive surveys of network modeling approaches. We differentiate somewhat more informally between three different forms of modeling that feature prominently in network analysis:

- The first consists of statistical models of associations between (network or non-network) variables but is not special to network analysis. This happens when the statistics involved may be obtained from networks via methods such as those described in Section 4.2 but are treated like any other quantity from then on. As an example of an important method that requires adaptation for relational data, we mention permutation tests (Krackhardt 1987; Dekker, Krackhardt, and Snijders 2007).
- The second class of models is used to describe the state or evolution of a network, often with networks as the dependent variables. Since statistical network models require their own kind of reasoning and are, therefore, special compared to other distributions, the remainder of this section is devoted to them.
- The third approach is simulation, in which likely outcomes are predicted from observed or deliberately chosen boundary conditions and assumptions about their influence. A prominent example is agent-based modeling in social simulation. Since these approaches are only

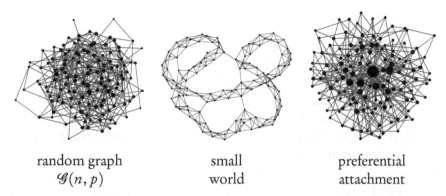

| random graph | small | preferential |
| $\mathcal{G}(n, p)$ | world | attachment |

Figure 34: Typical samples from simple models are highly artificial. All three have the same number of vertices and edges, and vertex size represents degree.

rarely used in empirical research, they are omitted from this book. Should you be interested in finding out more about them, we recommend Axelrod (1997) for an introduction to this domain.

A statistical network model consists of a set of conceivable network configurations together with a family of probability distributions on them. These distributions describe whether certain features shall be considered typical or atypical for a network. Typically, a parameterized family of distributions is specified (*modeling*) and a particular member of that family is selected based on an observed network (*estimation*). Whether features of the observation are significant is then assessed relative to the selected distribution. The role of the distribution is to represent variability in a population, measurement error, or uncertainty, and may, therefore, also be selected on other grounds. These general statements are made more concrete in the following.

4.3.1 Idealized Models

Let us start with basic models for the structure of simple, undirected graphs; no attributes, no directed edges considered. Although it is sometimes the case, the models presented in this section are not intended for use in empirical studies. Instead, they rather serve as idealized baseline models that illustrate a particular concept. Figure 34 shows anecdotal evidence that samples from these models are easily recognized as such.

Random Graphs

The number of vertices and the number of edges are two most straightforward features of a graph. We can define a statistical model on the class of all simple undirected graphs by postulating that all graphs with the same number of vertices and edges, n and m, are equally likely.

Given a simple undirected graph G that represents the structure of an observed network, the only reasonable choice of distribution from this model is the unique one with matching numbers of vertices and edges. Since empirical networks are, however, the result of a formation process that is usually far from being uniformly random, the expectation for features of graphs drawn from this distribution will be significantly different from those of the observed network structure. Loosely speaking, this is because a typical random graph has little variation in the density of any subgraph, i.e., almost no clustering, almost no deviation from average degrees, etc.

The study of random graphs is really a branch of mathematics, and it was neither initiated nor developed for the assessment of empirical phenomena but for showing the existence of graphs with certain structural characteristics, and the conditions under which they are rare or abundant. See Bollobás (2001) for a comprehensive treatment.

The model defined above is the original *Erdős-Rényi model* which we refer to as $\mathcal{G}(n, m)$. The more common variant, denoted $\mathcal{G}(n, p)$, is defined on the same class of graphs but with probability distributions parameterized by the number n of vertices and a common probability p for the existence of each individual edge (independent and identically distributed). From a mathematical perspective, these models are largely exchangable; for empirical purposes, they can serve as a no-knowledge baseline at best.

Small Worlds

The model of Watts and Strogatz (1998) confirms that it is possible to design graphs with structural features that seem plausible for social networks, namely overall sparseness, high local density, and short average distance.

This is achieved by starting from a cycle of n vertices, each of which is adjacent to its k nearest neighbors on the cycle for some small k, say $k = 6$. This highly artifical graph is sparse because k is chosen much smaller than n, and locally dense because most neighbors of a vertex are connected themselves. However, its diameter, the longest shortest path of any dyad, is large as it scales with $\frac{n}{k}$. The crucial observation is that even sparse random graphs have a low diameter because it is highly unlikely that none of the many possible shortcuts of a long shortest path is realized. Hence, when adding or rewiring a few edges at random, the average distance in this artificially constructed graph is reduced much faster than the other properties are lost.

Similar to random graphs, samples from this small-world model may have superficial similarity with graphs from observed networks, but, because of their sustained high degree of craftedness, they would yield a poor statistical model.

Preferential Attachment

Another frequent feature of observed network structures is the presence of vertices with high degree. Such vertices are very unlikely to feature in random graphs and small worlds, but they do appear in graphs sampled via a process proposed by Barabási and Albert (1999). In this process, a graph is constructed by starting from a small initial graph, to which more vertices are added one at a time. These are made adjacent with some k previously created vertices, where vertices with higher degree are more likely to be chosen as neighbors. This may be phrased as a tendency of new actors to attach themselves preferentially to already popular ones, increasing the popularity of the latter even further.

Even when the process appears plausible and the degree histogram of a preferential-attachment graph matches that of an observed structure fairly well, it would appear far-fetched to conclude that the actual formation process would have been similar. Like small worlds, preferential-attachment graphs only show that it is possible to construct graphs reproducing (insufficient) statistics.

Preferential attachment clearly yields graphs, in which vertex degrees generally decrease monotonically with creation time, and which are too clean and simple to reproduce more complex features generally found in empirical data.

4.3.2 Exponential-Family Random Graph Models

A family of models consisting of more general distributions is known as *exponential (family) random graph models* or simply the *ERGM* family.

They are defined on the class of all directed graphs with a fixed number of n vertices and, therefore, easily specialized to undirected graphs.

The probability distributions in ERGMs are from the exponential family, hence the name. Therefore, a graph G has probability $P(G) = \frac{1}{Z} \cdot e^{H(G)}$, where Z is a normalizing constant ensuring that the probabilities sum to one and H is any function assigning a number to each graph. Note that probabilities are monotone in H and that the model solely depends on the choice of H. To model the inherent complexity of real data while limiting the complexity of the form of H, H is restricted to linear combinations of any number of statistics (network-level indices), s_i, weighted by corresponding coefficients θ_i.

An ERGM thus has probability distributions

$$P(G) = \frac{1}{Z(\theta)} \cdot \exp\left\{ \sum_{i=1}^{k} \theta_i \cdot s_i(G) \right\}$$

for a fixed selection of statistics $s_1, \ldots, s_k$ and associated parameters $\theta = (\theta_1, \ldots, \theta_k)$. A straightforward example of a statistic is the edge count $m(G)$ and it can be checked that a $\mathcal{G}(n, p)$ random graph model is indeed a very simple ERGM with $H(G) = \left(\log \frac{p}{1-p} \right) \cdot m(G)$.

Typical ERGMs include $m(G)$ to control for density and then add several other substantively or otherwise meaningful statistics such as degrees, transitive triangles, or stars. In empirical research, model parameters θ are fitted to observed data. Parameter interpretation is not straightforward but this is a useful perspective: a parameter θ_i associated with statistic s_i measures the log-odds of forming an edge if that increases s_i by one, provided that the rest of the network remains constant.

As an example, let us consider the model used in Goodreau, Kitts, and Morris (2009) to investigate patterns of friendship formation among adolescents in the AddHealth data set (Resnick, Bearman, Blum, Bauman, Harris, Jones, Tabor, Beuhring, Sieving, Shew, Ireland, Bearinger, and Udry 1997). Three main factors are supposed to drive sociodemographic clustering, i.e., homophily in terms of sociodemographic attributes such as gender, race, or school grade.

The first factor is referred to as sociality, a personal characteristic, and included in the model as the total outdegree of all actors with the same attribute value for race, gender, and grade. The second factor is dyadic and called selective mixing. It is included by two types of statistics, the number of ties within groups of equal attribute values (gender) and the number of ties for each combination of two different attribute values (race and grade). The third factor is called triad closure and modeled by the so-called geometrically weighted edge-wise shared partner statistic (Hunter and Handcock 2006),

$$s_{\text{GWESP}}(G) = e^{\tau} \cdot \sum_{i=1}^{n-2} p_i(G) \left(1 - (1 - e^{\tau})^i\right) ,$$

where $p_i(G)$ counts the number of adjacent dyads with exactly i common neighbors and τ is a parameter modeling the decreasing marginal contribution of additional shared partners; the authors use $\tau = \frac{1}{4}$.

With total edge number and sociality complementing the sociodemographic variables as controls, Goodreau, Kitts, and Morris (2009) find evidence for both selective mixing and triadic closure, with hints at complex interaction effects. Disregarding the substantive results reported, the study illustrates nicely how relational models can be used to paint a more realistic picture of friendship formation. A more detailed introduction is provided in Robins, Pattison, Kalish, and Lusher (2007).

4.4 Summary

In principle, the analysis of networks is similar to the analysis of other, non-relational, data. However, for relations the unit of analysis is a dyad rather than a monad. Since dyads are heavily interdependent, and this interdependence is the actual substantive interest, other methods are required.

The link to an underlying network theory is best established through dyad indices because these evaluate the specific quality of relations between pairs of actors. Most methods essentially aggregate evaluations of particular dyads and they are generic in the sense that very often the dyad index can be chosen to account for a specific theoretical context.

While the methods of analysis discussed in Section 4.2 are often used for description, the quantities determined through them may also represent the core variables in inferential statistics. In addition, we have seen that modeling a population of networks, to which observations are contrasted, is a complex task and an area still under development.

We have deliberately omitted longitudinal networks because the inclusion of time leads to a combinatorial explosion of cases to consider. This is because different kinds of dynamics can be present in attributes, structure, composition, and processes taking place in a network, externalities, and any combination thereof, and with respect to any of the types of analysis discussed. Let us simply note that the usual first steps are time series analyses of the variables determined on cross-sectional snapshots of a longitudinal network and the *stochastic actor-oriented modeling* approach (Snijders et al. 2010).

4.5　Exercises

1. Assume that friendship network data was collected using a fixed-choice design, in which a class of 27 school children were asked to list up to five best friends from within the class in rank order. What can we conclude about density and average degree in the asymmetric network of nominations? How would that be different if the boundary was specified as including all 234 children in the entire school, or in a free-choice questionnaire design?

2. Consider any undirected graph $G = (V, E)$. The so-called *Handshake Lemma* is a formal statement which asserts that the sum of all degrees is twice the number of edges, $\sum_{i \in V} \deg(i) = 2m$. Argue that this holds for all undirected graphs. Argue also, that the number of guests at a party who shake hands with an odd number of other guests is even, and that there are at least two guests who shake hands with the exact same number of other guests (although not necessarily with the same other guests).

3. Given a population sample of m men and f women, let the relation "is or has been married to" be represented in a rectangular $m \times f$-matrix with entries in the range $\{0, 1\}$.

   - What are the disadvantages of this two-mode network representation?

   - What is the maximum number of 3-cliques in such a network?

   - If we use a one-mode network representation instead, what are the dimensions of the corresponding adjacency matrix?

4. List all possible triad types for undirected networks.

5. A dyad consists of two actors and allows for two different orderings. Similarly, a triad consists of three actors and allows for six different orderings. Discuss why triadic configurations in dyadic data form a special case of *triadic data*, and give an example of triadic data that cannot be represented as triads of a network. Come up with two definitions of your own for what might be called *three-mode data* and discuss the differences.

6. Why is closeness centrality ill-defined on (directed) graphs that are not (strongly) connected? Can you think of alternative centrality measures that are based on the same idea but applicable to any (directed) graph?

7. It is often observed that random graphs and graphs with a core-periphery structure yield highly correlated values for degree, closeness, and betweenness centrality. Can you explain this finding? Construct a small undirected graph in which the most central vertices according to degree, closeness and betweenness are all different.

8. Why do structurally equivalent vertices have the same eigenvector centrality? Does this also hold for vertices that are regular equivalent?

9. Explain why graphs with the same triad census can have different clustering coefficient distributions. Give an example.

10. Give lower and upper bounds on the number of edges in the k-core of an undirected graph. Can you do the same for a clique of k vertices?

11. What is the difference between the triad census and the coefficients of triadic statistics in ERGMs?

12. Consider an ERGM for graphs with $n = 42$ vertices. Let the edge count $m(G)$ be its only statistic $s_1(G)$ with corresponding parameter $\theta_1 = -0.7$. Which graph has maximum probability, and what is (roughly) the expected number of edges of a graph sampled from this distribution?

5 Visualization

Social network diagrams are helpful for exploring and presenting your data. This is because, more than sequential text or data tables that are difficult to memorize, diagrams can communicate information in context, with many potentially interesting relationships represented simultaneously.

After reading this chapter, you will know how to start thinking about the design of a visualization, and which are the most important choices you will face. You will have some general guidelines available for the routine production of visualizations, and you will also know how to critically review the results. Like any of the other approaches discussed in this book, visualization is a tool that requires serious consideration. Visualizations that display analytical results in the context of the data that led to them are usually the best way to boost confidence in a finding.

Visualization is an indispensable tool in data analysis because the human visual system with its high bandwidth and pattern recognition capabilities facilitates the in-take of information in parallel and in context.

Purposefully crafted visualizations can be an enormous help in *exploring* collected data and analytical results. In particular, they may ease the identification of trends, outliers, transitions, systematic errors, implausible configurations, and other types of patterns. In this scenario, visualization is a tool used by researchers to obtain a better grasp of their data and to boost confidence in their findings. This may be especially valuable if the analysis rests on computer-implemented methods which produce aggregate results that are difficult to check for correctness.

For much the same reasons, visualization can also be effective for *presenting* results in a comprehensible and memorizable way. While graphical representations can be just as persuasive, misleading, or confusing as written text, they can also be enlightening, convincing, and reassuring for readers trying to follow the ideas of the originator. Ideally, they can provide an iconic summary of the findings, to which a careful analysis has led.

To exploit the power of visualization, however, it is crucial to realize that graphic communication requires the same care and consideration as textual communication, only with different means of expression and with different pitfalls to avoid. Paraphrasing Brandes, Kenis, Raab, Schneider, and Wagner (1999), the construction of network diagrams can be broken down into three essential tasks:

Identify relevant information: Obviously, the elementary pieces of data make up an important part of the information to be conveyed. A network visualization should therefore facilitate the identification of direct and indirect linkages. In addition, there may be actor and tie attributes that should also be visualized, and there may be known or unknown dependencies between any of these data.

Beyond the plain data, however, there is also a more indirect type of information that is equally, if not more important. Network visualizations are generally produced in a particular analytical context. The information relevant to the interests of the reader should, therefore, also be considered by the producer (who may be the same person). Common examples include the differential structural importance of actors or cohesive groups.

Choose an appropriate graphic design: Once we know which type of information is relevant, we should design a visualization that will show this information in the most undistorted and comprehensible way. The choices to be made include not only the graphical elements for each unit of information, but also layout, shapes, colors, etc. The main criteria are accuracy (effectiveness), ease-of-reading (efficency), and joy-of-reading (aesthetics). It is also a good idea to check for conventions, traditions, and viewing expectations that intended readers may have.

These goals are often contradictory, and we may be constrained further by limited support from software tools, for instance. Fortunately, there are some simple and fairly general design principles that you can apply. We will discuss them throughout this chapter.

Understand the results: More often than not, you will require the help of software tools to produce a design. Automated computation is the default, at least for the spatial arrangement of graphical elements and the mapping of data to graphical attributes such as size.

The interplay between certain design choices and algorithmically produced graphics can be quite complex, however. Algorithms may introduce artifacts, and unintended results are produced regularly when an outcome is suggestive for a type of information that was not part of the design or is not addressed in the algorithmic realization. For example, it is often the case that structurally peripheral actors are located near the center of a diagram produced by standard network layout algorithms because these algorithms do not account for any particular type of centrality. Because of the suggestive nature of visual representations, it is, therefore, important to understand which features of a particular type of diagram can be interpreted reliably.

5.1 Graphical Representation

Design is choice, and the first choice to be made is how to graphically represent the units of information. Fortunately, as we will see, you can choose between two standard packages for the most part.

The elements of a network are actors, ties, labels, and numbers. The elements of a diagram are points, lines, areas, and text. Before we can even think about how to choose a layout, colors, shapes, etc. in a diagram, we have to specify which type of graphical element is used for which type of network element; this specification is the choice of representation.

We will discuss two representations that are most frequently used, the sociogram and the sociomatrix, below. Choosing between these two types of representation is made easy by some simple guidelines. While alternatives exist, these are not at all common in the context of social networks. Conventions for representing two-mode networks are much looser, which is why we discuss them separately at the end of this section.

5.1.1 Sociogram

Sociograms are instances of standard representations for graphs, in which vertices are represented by point-like graphical objects and edges by line-like graphical objects. These are sometimes referred to as *point-and-line representations*, *ball-and-stick representations*, or *node-link diagrams*. They were common, for instance, in drawings of family trees or illustrations in the mathematical literature long before their first systematic use in the social sciences.

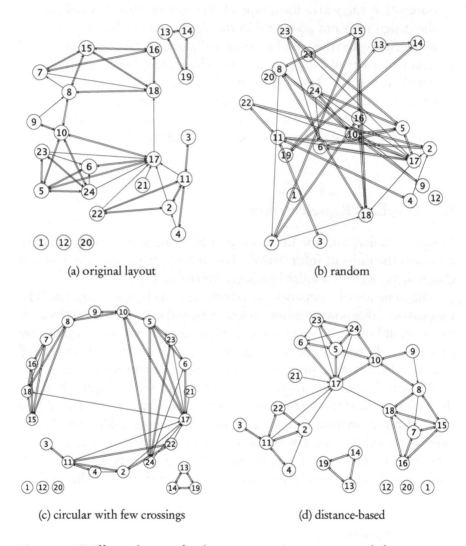

(a) original layout

(b) random

(c) circular with few crossings

(d) distance-based

Figure 35: Different layouts for the same acquaintance network from Moreno (1953: 145).

Once the type of representation has been decided on, the question arises as to how to design a "good" diagram? As illustrated in Figure 35, the positioning of actors governs readability to a large extent. If bent or curved lines are allowed, the routing of ties becomes another important factor. As far back as the 1930s, Moreno (1953: 141) suggested that "the number of line crossings be minimized" and that "the existence of subgroups should be observable;" he presents the diagram in Figure 35(a) as a good example.

The computer-assisted layout of Figure 35(d) fares even better with respect to the visual separation of cohesive groups. This is mainly due to more uniform edge lengths and an improved display of symmetries. The number of crossings, however, is not minimal (try rearranging the nodes yourself).

We briefly review the main principles of the underlying layout algorithm to better understand and interpret automatically produced layouts of sociograms. It should be noted that almost all software tools for network analysis feature similar layout algorithms, although many implementations exhibt some notable deficiencies due to seemingly minor differences in the algorithm.

A core observation is that instead of targeting difficult and mostly contradicting layout objectives explictly, we can focus on one single principle – representation of structural distance – that turns out to also address, explicitly or implicitly, the others. Typical layout objectives are based on general properties of the data,

- variation in the density of nodes in the layout should reflect varying cohesion in structure,
- variation in distance between pairs of nodes should reflect varying graph-theoretic distances,
- variation in the length of lines should reflect varying tie values, and
- geometric symmetries should reflect structural symmetries,

and also on general readability criteria,

- nodes should not overlap,
- lines should not cross,
- lines should not pass through nodes, and
- angles between incident or crossing lines should be large.

The striking observation is that accurate representation of shortest-path distances yields layouts for which also the other criteria are satisfied reasonably well. For instance, actors in a cohesive group will be placed closer together because many of them are directly connected, whereas actors not belonging to the group have larger distances to at least some group members and will thus be placed farther away from them.

Even with distance representation as the only criterion there are many alternative implementations. Most software tools today rely on algorithms referred to as *spring embedders* (Eades 1984; Fruchterman and Reingold 1991; Brandes 2001). These build on the metaphor of mutually repelling nodes that are held together by springs if there is an edge between them. Due to this binary criterion (linked or not linked) and the algorithmically challenging problem of minimizing the tension in this virtual system, satisfactory results are obtained reliably only for small and sparse networks.

More accurate and reliable results are obtained by considering indirect linkages with their actual distance rather than with uniform repulsive forces. Representing these graph-theoretic distances in a low dimensional space, such as the two or three-dimensional layout space, is an instance of multidimensional scaling, which, in turn, is a well-studied problem (France and Carroll 2011), for which reliable and scalable implementations exist. In fact, some of the first automated approaches to social network visualization were based on it (Kruskal and Seery 1980).

Historically, the first variant of multidimensional scaling is what is now called *classical scaling* (Torgerson 1952; Gower 1966) and sometimes referred to as *metric scaling*. The mathematical basis is spectral decomposition of a matrix derived from input dissimilarities. For shortest-path distances of a graph, the effect is that large distances dominate the outcome (providing for a good spread of the network) and that nodes with very similar distances to others are placed close together (graphically conveying near structural equivalence). Moreover, the results are essentially unique and thus reproducible.

Brandes and Pich (2009) argue that the best distance representations are obtained from *distance scaling* (Shepard 1962; Kruskal 1964), in which the objective is to minimize a weighted version of the squared error in distance representation. In a nutshell, distance scaling is an approach for fitting layout distances to shortest-path distances by iteratively moving nodes to improve the fit. It is very dependent on the initial configuration, since it is difficult to improve representation of large distances during this iteration. The implementation commonly recommended is to start from a classical scaling layout (which represents large distances well) so that only local configurations need to be improved during distance scaling iterations. This approach can be implemented so that it scales to very large graphs with millions of nodes and edges.

If nothing else is known about the network, and no other information is required to be conveyed via node positions, distance scaling is, therefore, the preferred method for computing a layout. Consequently, it is also the method of choice for an initial exploration of network data prior to further analysis.

5.1.2   Sociomatrix

While a sociogram with node positions determined by distance scaling should be considered as the default approach to social network visualization, there are situations with straightforward characteristics, in which another representation, the *sociomatrix*, is preferrable.

A sociomatrix is a matrix, in which each cell contains a graphical element signifying the value of the corresponding dyadic variable. An early example with a three-valued dyad attribute is shown in Figure 36.

The obvious advantage is in the straightfoward location of each piece of dyadic information. This avoids the cluttering of sociograms, particularly for dense and valued networks. Like the sociogram, the readability of the sociomatrix depends on its layout whereby the layout of a matrix is the ordering of its rows and columns. This degree of freedom was first exploited in archaeology for sequencing artifacts (Petrie 1899; Robinson 1951). Its use for data visualization was promoted in Bertin (1983) using the concept of "the reorderable matrix."

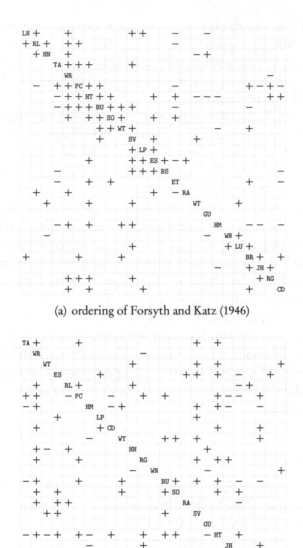

(a) ordering of Forsyth and Katz (1946)

(b) random ordering

*Figure 36: Two sociomatrices displaying the same network of attraction ("+")
and repulsion ("−") among a group of school girls living in the same cot-
tage (Moreno 1953). The random alternative stresses the dependency of group
visibility on the order of rows and columns.*

Again, many criteria exist for the ordering of rows and columns. An obvious one is the name-inducing block-wise ordering in blockmodeling, in which the elements of a block are made contiguous. A special case of blockmodeling is the partition of a network into a cohesive core and a loosely connected periphery.

The dominant criterion for ordering a matrix representation, however, is a generalization of the core-periphery blockmodel. By arranging the actors in such a way that their structural neighbors are also close in the ordering, cohesive groups form contiguous intervals and, therefore, dense blocks on the diagonal of the sociomatrix as in Figure 36(a). Since, once again, there is no universally good ordering, the results should only be interpreted in terms of confirmation: If blocks can be observed, their members form a cohesive group – however it is very difficult to conclude anything about the absence of such structures by looking at a diagram because they may just be hidden in a poor ordering as in Figure 36(b).

The two most striking visual features that a sociomatrix can produce are dense blocks and cross-like patterns caused by high-degree actors. The latter suggests that we can also exploit the alignment in rows and columns for trends and outlier detection. An example, in which the fixed location of dyads and the alignment of related dyads are exploited is provided in Figure 37.

Advantages and disadvantages of sociograms and sociomatrices have been discussed in various arenas (Moreno 1946; Katz 1947; Ghoniem, Fekete, and Castagliola 2005). We offer the following general guidelines in conclusion:

- Sociograms are more suitable for sparse networks
  and the investigation of indirect linkages.
- Sociomatrices are more suitable for dense networks
  and the investigation of partition blocks.

Not surprisingly, combinations that capitalize on the best of both worlds have been attempted (Henry, Fekete, and McGuffin 2007), however, for now at least, they have not become common practice. Matrix representations rarely feature in software tools in general.

Figure 37: Matrix representation of the Newcomb Fraternity data (cf. Box 13) from Brandes and Nick (2011). In each cell, the 15 mutual rankings are represented as tilted bars in a see-saw design, time-ordered from bottom to top. Two-sided preference and asymmetry in a dyad are depicted as length and tilting angle, so that, say, a weakly reciprocated preference of a row actor results in a left-heavy bar. The top three choices of each actor are highlighted in black, and the darkness of nodes indicates deviation from average popularity. Two notable blocks along the diagonal correspond to two cohesive groups that are relatively stable over time.

Box 19: The Southern Women

For a study of racial segregation and social stratification in the south of the USA, two couples, one white and one black, immersed themselves into the local society of a town in the state of Mississippi. The Davises and the Gardners collected various data in participatory field observation in the 1930s. The two-mode data set of joint attendance of 18 women in 14 social events (Davis et al. 1941: 148) has become particularly famous because it clearly demonstrated the existence of social cliques that have since been rediscovered using countless clustering methods (Freeman 2003).

5.1.3 Two-Mode Network Representations

Two-mode networks are not a form of graphical representation but a particular type of network data. Because of their greater generality, however, they lend themselves to even more alternative representations than the sociogram and sociomatrix discussed for one-mode networks above. Adaptations of these standard representations to the two-mode scenario are exemplified in Figure 38.

An alternative view of two-mode networks is the interpretation of the elements of one mode as defining subsets of the elements of the other mode. As was already pointed out in Chapter 4 this interpretation yields a hypergraph representation. A common graphical representation of hypergraphs uses point-like objects for vertices (the elements of one mode) and areas enclosing all incident vertices for hyperedges (the elements of the other mode). See Figure 39(a) for an example.

It may be difficult, and even impossible for more complex configurations, to realize such a representation as, in order for the layout to be unambiguous, it is essential that any vertex not contained in a hyperedge be located outside of the corresponding area. This is just one reason why few software tools support hypergraph diagrams using the subset representation.

Another alternative is to focus on representing the inclusion relations between the sets of incidences. This representation is illustrated in Figure 39(b) as a Galois lattice and reflects the duality of the two modes very well (Freeman and White 1993). To read it, note that any dot represents a pair of subsets of women and events with the following property: Each woman in the set has attended each of the events (and, by duality, vice

participants × events	A	B	C	D	E	F	G	H	I	J	K	L	M	N
1. Mrs. Evelyn Jefferson	×	×	×	×	×	×	.	×	×	.	.	.	.	.
2. Ms. Laura Mandeville	×	×	×	.	×	×	×	×	.	.	.	.	.	.
3. Ms. Theresa Anderson	.	×	×	×	×	×	×	×	×	.	.	.	.	.
4. Ms. Brenda Rogers	×	.	×	×	×	×	×	×	.	.	.	.	.	.
5. Ms. Charlotte McDowd	.	.	×	×	×	.	×	.	.	.	.	.	.	.
6. Ms. Frances Anderson	.	.	×	.	×	×	.	×	.	.	.	.	.	.
7. Ms. Eleanor Nye	.	.	.	.	×	×	×	×	.	.	.	.	.	.
8. Ms. Pearl Oglethorpe	.	.	.	.	.	×	.	×	×	.	.	.	.	.
9. Ms. Ruth DeSand	.	.	.	.	×	.	×	×	×	.	.	.	.	.
10. Ms. Verne Sanderson	.	.	.	.	.	.	×	×	×	.	.	×	.	.
11. Ms. Myra Liddell	.	.	.	.	.	.	.	×	×	×	.	×	.	.
12. Ms. Katherine Rogers	.	.	.	.	.	.	.	×	×	×	.	×	×	×
13. Mrs. Sylvia Avondale	.	.	.	.	.	.	×	×	×	×	.	×	×	×
14. Mrs. Nora Fayette	.	.	.	.	.	×	×	.	×	×	×	×	×	×
15. Mrs. Helen Lloyd	.	.	.	.	.	.	×	×	.	×	×	×	.	.
16. Mrs. Dorothy Murchison	.	.	.	.	.	.	.	×	×	.	.	.	.	.
17. Mrs. Olivia Carleton	.	.	.	.	.	.	.	.	×	.	×	.	.	.
18. Mrs. Flora Price	.	.	.	.	.	.	.	.	×	.	×	.	.	.

(a) two-mode (rectangular) sociomatrix

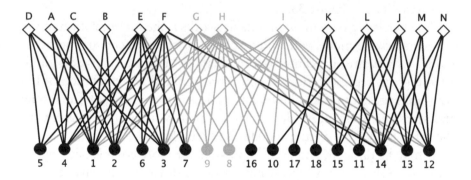

(b) two-mode (two-layer) sociogram

Figure 38: Graphical representations adapted for two-mode networks. The sociomatrix of Davis et al. (1941) is not square but rectangular, with rows indexed by one mode and columns indexed by the other. The sociogram is organized in a two-layer layout with an ordering resulting in few line crossings. The cohesion-driven orderings make it possible to highlight an almost perfect separation into two camps that is bridged by two women and three events.

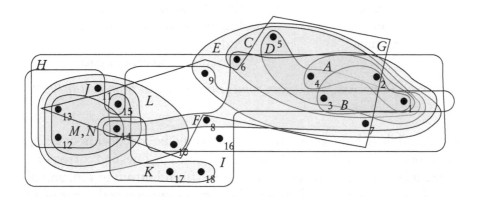

(a) events as subsets

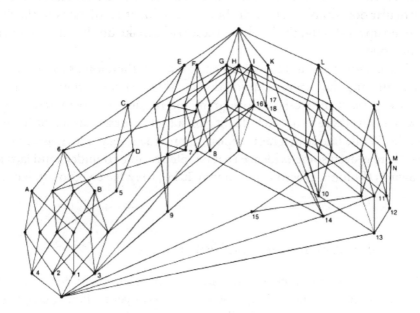

(b) Galois lattice (reproduced from Freeman and White 1993)

Figure 39: Alternative representations of the network from Figure 38.

graphical elements	graphical variables
point	x-, y-, z-coordinates
curve	size, shape, orientation,
area	brightness, color, transparency
volume	texture
	movement and other dynamics

Figure 40: Primitives for diagram composition (adapted from Bertin 1983).

versa), and there is no woman or event that could be added without losing this property. Set inclusion relations are depicted by lines and correspond to the union of sets of women when going from bottom to top, and of sets of events from top to bottom. The top dot represents the pair of all women and no event, whereas the bottom dot represents the pair of no woman and all events. To find out which women are represented in a particular dot, simply start at the bottom and identify all paths to the dot that are upward only; the labels on these paths make up the set of women being sought.

Exchanging the roles of women and events is, therefore, simply a matter of turning the diagram upside down. While corresponding dualities are also present in two-layer sociogram and rectangular sociomatrix representations, there is no such duality in subset representations of hypergraphs. While lattice diagrams appear to provide a very informative view and there is even some evidence that people are able to understand lattice drawings (Eklund, Ducrou, and Brawn 2004), they have yet to catch on.

5.2   Multivariate Information Visualization

The representations in the previous section define the language we plan to use for visual communication, however, we have yet to find appropriate expressions for our content. While the following discussion assumes that we are designing a sociogram, you are encouraged to think about how to apply similar techniques to other representations as well.

Having identified the type of informationi that should be conveyed graphically, a translation of data variables into graphical features is sought. How do we decide on this translation? The choice of representation constrains the use of graphical elements but we are largely free in how we assign values to the graphical variables listed in Figure 40. Should the degree of an actor be depicted by the size of the corresponding node, for example? Or should we use a color gradient? What if we wish to gain insight into the relation between degree and another attribute such as gender? The answer is, of course: It depends. While we cannot resolve the general problems of statistical graphics here, we can point to some useful criteria and strategies.

Two elementary criteria are the level of measurement of a data variable and the accuracy, with which humans perceive variation in a graphical variable. In Figure 41, graphical variables are ranked according to how accurately humans perceive data at standard levels of measurement. Obviously, several distinct graphical attributes have to be used to depict several data attributes, and these rankings help with matching and prioritizing.

Since position is the most accurately perceived graphical variable, we devote special attention to constrained network layouts in the next section before we consider mapping more data to other graphical variables. In the final section of this chapter we are going to discuss ways of reducing information in visual representations in situations, in which the size or resolution of the display space is too small or the amount of information is distracting.

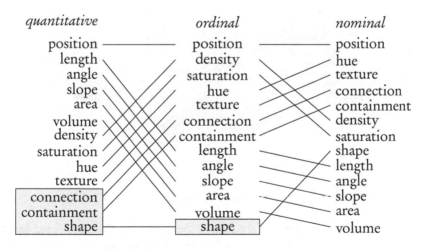

Figure 41: Perception accuracy (decreasing top to bottom) of data mapped to graphical variables, where boxes indicate variables irrelevant for this type of data (redrawn from Mackinlay 1986).

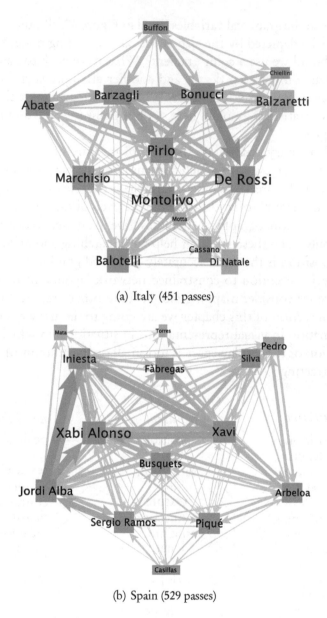

(a) Italy (451 passes)

(b) Spain (529 passes)

Figure 42: Networks of completed passes in the UEFA EURO 2012 final Spain vs. Italy (official data). Node height/width represents number of passes received/given, substitute players are depicted in lighter color; edge width and saturation represent the number of passes. Layouts are according to tactical lineups.

5.2.1   Substance-Based Layout

As we have argued that network visualization begins with the identification of relevant information and have seen that positions offer the most accurate means of depicting data values, we shall now look at alternative approaches to designing the layout of a network diagram. Hence, we would like to use our best means for the most important information. In the following subsections, we discuss four important layout schemes that adapt the recommended design for general networks to particular types of substantive information.

Mapped Coordinates

Location data extrinsic to the network may provide important contextual information. Examples of this kind include geographical coordinates, tactical formations in team sports, or a reader's mental maps formed by previously viewed diagrams and maps. Since there are many situations, in which relations exist between spatial and structural proximity, the joint visualization of these two types of information makes it easier to inspect or communicate such relations.

Figure 42 shows an example of an interaction network, in which interactions between spatially close actors are more frequent than between distant actors. As illustrated by substituted players, readability may be improved by moving actors slightly to avoid occlusion, if locations only need to be represented qualitatively.

In other cases, the essential information may be contained in other attribute data that are numerical, but do not have a spatial interpretation. The network in Figure 43 is overlayed on a two-dimensional scatterplot of the actors. Since, in general, the coordinate-defining attributes will not be ideal for readability of the network, it may be necessary to move some labels and bend some edges to reduce overlap.

Status

The use of the y-axis to represent a status index is a particular example of non-spatial data mapped to coordinates. Such visualizations appeal to the common notion of "high" and "low" status. Since only one dimension is fixed by the attribute, the remaining degree of freedom along the x-axis can be used to improve readability, for example by applying a constrained layout algorithm.

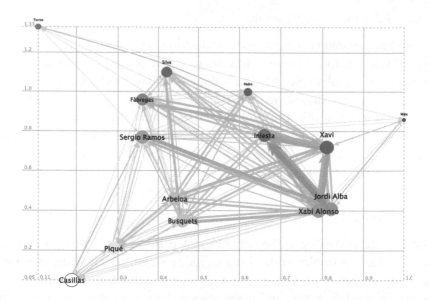

Figure 43: Network of Figure 42(b) in a scatterplot layout (x: passes given per 90min, y: passes received per 90min). Node area corresponds to minutes played, saturation to passing involvement (passes given and received per 90min).

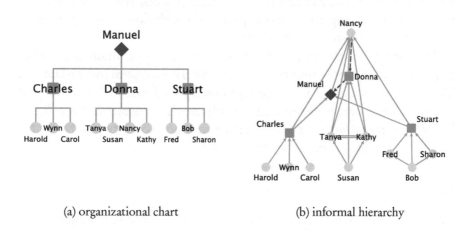

(a) organizational chart   (b) informal hierarchy

Figure 44: An advice network revealing that the informal hierachy in a business unit differs from the formal one (adapted from Krackhardt 1996). On the right, vertical coordinates are fixed according to a status index.

This substance-based design is the default for organizational charts but it also applies to other structural hierarchies. Its effectiveness is demonstrated by the example in Figure 44, where the formal hierarchy given by the organizational chart and the informal hierarchy given by an advice-seeking relation differ considerably.

Centrality

Another type of network-related information that is technically the same, but has a slightly different connotation, is centrality. The immediate visual metaphor relates centrality to the center of a diagram. Mapping an actor attribute to distance from the center corresponds exactly to the above approach for status, the only difference being that instead of Cartesian (x- and y-) coordinates we use polar (radius and angle) coordinates. Again, one dimension (radius) is fixed, and the other can be used to improve readability, e.g., by arranging the nodes such that the number of crossings is low.

In Figure 45, the radial dimension represents two actor indices, namely the geodesic distance from the instructor and the president, respectively, of a karate club (Zachary 1977). The group split over views regarding the price of lessons, and it is quite apparent that the decision of members to go with either of the two opponents is largely a function of whom they are closer to. No sophisticated clustering analysis is needed to explain this separation.

It should be noted that the graphic interpretation of distance from a focal point is also very common in ego network maps (cf. the example in Figure 2).

Grouping

We have argued that a good network layout should match variation in cohesion by variation in layout density, and that structural proximity should result in layout proximity. The underlying rationale is that, according to gestalt theory, humans perceive relatively close objects as a group.

If groups are not induced by structural cohesion, the same principles can still be applied. The layout of the network in Figure 6 was determined by classical scaling (Section 5.1.1) and, therefore, groups nodes that correspond to actors with similar relations to others (near structural equivalence). Similar impressions of meta-edges are obtained from any role assignment.

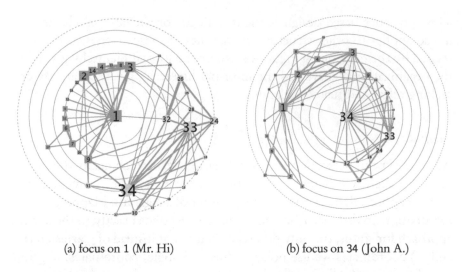

(a) focus on 1 (Mr. Hi)   (b) focus on 34 (John A.)

Figure 45: Centrality visualizations focusing on key figures in in interaction network from Zachary (1977). Line thickness represents number of interaction contexts, layout distance from focal nodes represents shortest-path distance. Since node shapes corresponds to membership in newly formed groups after a split, the drawings communicate that proximity to either of the faction leaders explains alignment almost perfectly, and that 9 is an interesting actor to investigate further.

Even if groups are defined extrinsic to the network with no structural correspondence, geometric grouping can serve to relate a network to other forms of organization. For example, the boundaries of hierarchically organized business units may be drawn into an image of email communication among their members. An example in which extrinsic grouping is traded-off against structural cohesion is given in Figure 49. Here, countries were placed first by continent and then automatically rearranged one continental group at a time with the others fixed. Some manual readability improvements were performed in a postprocessing stage. Interestingly, some continental groups were separated because of their different trade relations with other parts of the world.

In all of the above layout schemes node positions are limited to conveying network structure in the context of additional or derived attribute data. The governing principle is to represent the attribute information precisely (hard constraint), for example by fixing one dimension according to an attribute, and to use the remaining degrees of freedom to improve readability (soft constraint, objective). When deviating from the general-purpose layout based on representation of shortest-path distances, two things must, therefore, be considered: Is there an accurate and intuitive geometric representation for the information of interest, and to what extent can the criteria for readable layout (cf. p. 154) still be satisfied?

5.2.2 Other Graphical Variables

Graphical variables other than position are easier to control in the sense that there are fewer dependencies between them in the data and they do not require sophisticated layout algorithms. Nevertheless, the problem of design choices remains.

The decision as to which data attribute to map to which graphical variable, and how, is mostly specific to the combination of available data, relevant derived information, and substantive interest. Hence there is no catalog of universally appropriate mappings from which to choose. While we offer a few guidelines in Box 21 at the end of this chapter, these should be critically re-evaluated for the context, in which they are applied.

5.3 Information Layering

Although it is generally advisable to utilize multivariate information visualization to allow for triangulation and within-data comparison, display space is limited by size and resolution. As a result, clutter and noise may hide even a clear signal. Moreover, the sheer amount of information may cause disorientation and confusion. Hence, we will now discuss three related general strategies that may help alleviate these problems:

- *Filtering* is used to reduce the amount of information by omitting less relevant data;
- *level of detail* visualizations show smaller networks obtained by aggregation and/or filtering; and
- *micro/macro* visualizations display multiple levels of detail simultaneously in one diagram.

Common to all these strategies is the creation of layers of information as an organization principle.

Box 20: The World Trade Network

From a statistical analysis of bilateral and multilateral trade flows, Rose (2004) concludes that the General Agreement on Tariffs and Trade (GATT) and later the World Trade Organization (WTO) may have had no effect on trading volumes between member countries. In their subsequent work, Subramanian and Wei (2007) focus on the longitudinal network of bilateral trade and conclude that WTO membership does promote trade but conditional on the level of development and membership history of the countries involved, as well as the economic sector.

Like previous work, these studies employ a *gravity model*, in which trade flows are predicted from country attributes such as gross domestic product and tie attributes such as geographic distances. Some additional network analyses and visualizations can be found in De Benedictis and Tajoli (2011).

5.3.1   Filtering

A straightforward solution to the problem of too much data is to forget about some of it. While this may sound rather crude, it may in fact be completely viable if, for example, the excluded data has little or no influence on the results. Let us look at an example that illustrates this point.

The country-level trade data analyzed in Subramanian and Wei (2007) gives rise to a network of $m = 11,938$ trade relationships between $n = 157$ countries for the year 2000. Hence, the density is almost 50% with average indegree and outdegree greater than 76. For graphs with high density and, therefore, very probably also low diameter, the standard layout advocated in Section 5.1.1 is unreadable. Drawings like the one in Figure 46 are often ridiculed as "hairballs."

Even though they are depicted equally, the relationships are actually valued by trade volume, and can be considered, therefore, as being of differential importance for global trade. Import/export volumes between pairs of countries range from 58 to $1,331,021,440$ US\$ with rapidly declining frequencies. Thresholding at $1,000,000$ US\$ removes 84 percent of the links and results in a network that is much easier to layout (see Figure 47. While the main trade flows are preserved, many smaller economies have become isolated because they do not maintain any trading relationship exceeding the threshold.

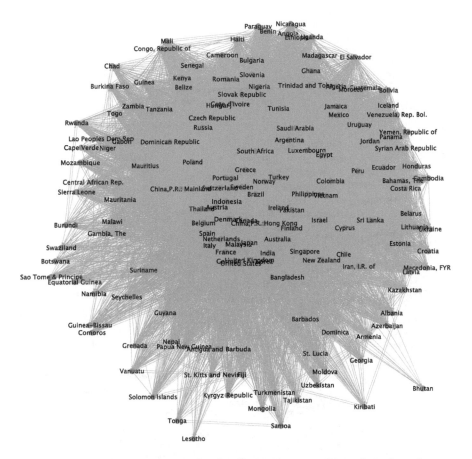

Figure 46: World trade network of Subramanian and Wei (2007) with standard layout and no attribute data shown.

One way to keep small economies in the system is to apply individual thresholds and retain the top k trading relationships of each country instead. For Figure 48 we chose $k = 7$ because with this choice the same number of links that are kept is almost exactly the same as in Figure 47. Apparently the distribution is very different, though. This time we may have lost some strong trading relationships that can be considered important on the global level but are not among the most important for the two countries involved. As a result some larger economies have become peripheral because of the specific pattern of their retained ties to the center and a concentrated periphery.

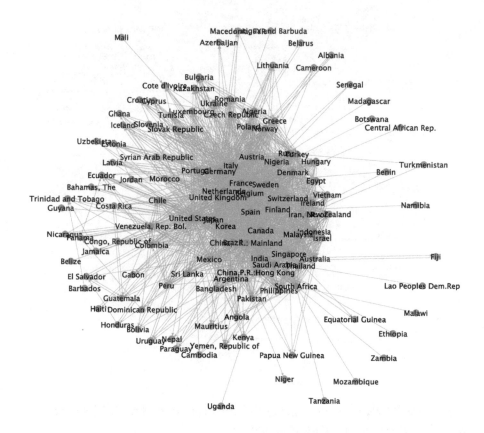

Figure 47: World trade relationships with a minimum of 1,000,000 US$. While the network appears to be more readable, many countries have become disconnected.

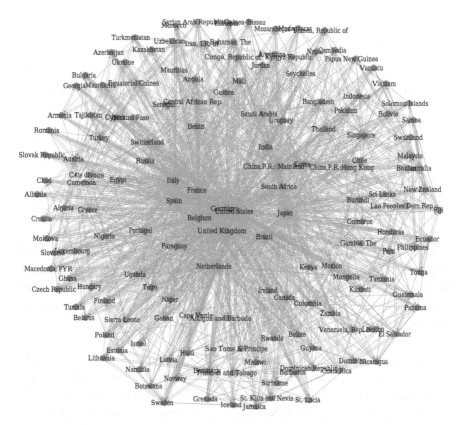

Figure 48: Retaining only the seven most important import and export relations for each country preserves the core-periphery divide of the world trade network but fails to show other structure.

As a variant of filtering, we would like to note that highlighting and greying out are alternative ways of focusing attention without actually omitting data. In Figure 38(b) we made use of this technique to depict the network both with and without a select group of women and events without duplication. In fact, this technique can be generalized for the separation of information that is filtered using different criteria into groups visualized using different color, strokes, fonts, etc. Tufte (1983) is a great source of inspiration on this.

5.3.2   Level of Detail

An alternative to filtering data based on relevance is aggregation, whereby parts of the data that are not sufficiently relevant by themselves are summarized and depicted in larger units. The level of detail shown might, but does not have to, depend on a zoom level, at which part of the network is displayed.

We exemplify this approach using hierarchical actor classifications as the means of defining successively smaller and more abstract versions of a network. To move from one level of detail to the next coarser one, actors in the same class are merged into a group node, and all of their relations to actors in some class (including their own) are aggregated into a group tie. This network-transforming operation is usually referred to as *contraction by attribute*, and is reversed when changing from some level of detail to the next finer one. The concrete form of aggregation depends on the type of data associated with ties. In the world trade network, the trade relations of countries in the same class are reasonably aggregated by adding up the individual trade volumes. For relations such as frequency of contact, averaging may be more suitable.

Note that the world trade network is an aggregation on an already very high level because each import/export volume relation summarizes many individual deals between companies and institutions, over a certain time period and by country. We can abstract the network further by aggregating these countries according to, e.g., geo-political region, political system, or level of development. All of these yield hierarchical classifications of actors based on attribute data that is extrinsic to the structure.

Levels of detail can also be defined in structural terms. A straightforward method for summarizing the main structural differences is hierarchical clustering based on cohesion. It should be noted, however, that every blockmodel also yields a summarization, and that the image matrix of a blockmodel is indeed a level-of-detail visualization in the sociomatrix representation.

A more general approach to defining levels of detail is called *semantic zooming*. It can be interpreted as a combination of filtering and aggregation, whereby details other than those that result from disaggregating a higher-level view are presented only from a certain sufficiently fine level. In the world trade network, for instance, it may not be interesting or even reasonable to display attributes such as political system on some aggregate level, whereas this may be relevant information on the country level. Likewise, value-based filters can be made dependent on the level of detail.

While it is recognized that higher levels of abstraction generally create ambiguities due to aggregation and filtering, a less considered consequence is that contractions typically yield denser networks that are more difficult to layout.

5.3.3 Micro/Macro Reading

If complexity or actual levels of interest rather than limitations of the visualization media are the motivation for defining levels of detail, we do not have to create multiple visualizations just because, conceptually, we are creating multiple views. Instead, we can use these levels to organize a single visualization such that it can be read at multiple levels.

The term *micro/macro readings* was coined by Tufte (1990) and suggests that at least two scales are present: a macro level, at which broad features in the data can be recognized, and a micro level, at which the elementary data are presented. It is like seeing both the forest *and* the trees.

The main advantage is that detailed information is presented in the context of the bigger picture. Apparent features of the aggregate data thus provide a frame of reference, and allow for comparison across scales. Being able to do this in a single diagram is presumably less disruptive than across multiple visualizations.

But one way of applying this principle is demonstrated in Figure 49. Given a regional aggregation of the world trade network, we can take positions from an upscaled version of a regional-level drawing into account when computing a layout for the country-level network, for example by introducing invisible region nodes, to which member country nodes should be proximate. This creates extra space around region boundaries and thus helps with the recognition of regions as higher-level units. In this diagram, however, we have taken a different approach by running a layout algorithm restricted to one group at a time, with the other groups and the biggest economy of the current group fixed. While this yields fairly similar results in general, it allows for groups to split if they are attached to different subnetworks.

Nodes represent countries and their height and width corresponds to the total import and export volumes. Node boundaries are drawn to ease perception of deviations from a square which would indicate a trade

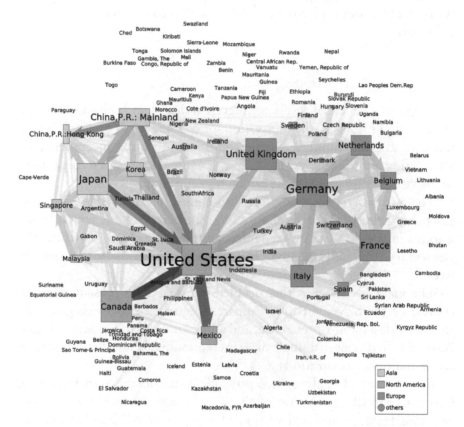

Figure 49: The world trade network of Subramanian and Wei (2007) with layers of information and a micro/macro design. The layout partially preserves continental groupings and sizes indicate trade volume, both for nodes and edges. Height and width of nodes corresponds to total import and export volume (indegree vs. outdegree), so that nodes that are higher than wide correspond to countries with a trade deficit.

imbalance. Asian, European, and North-American countries are distinguished by grey level, whereas all other countries have a ellipse-shaped node. Label sizes correspond to total trade volume (sum of import and export), but are shifted by an added constant to reduce the ratio between smallest and largest label font.

Instead of filtering edges out, we vary both their width and color by the trade volume attribute. To avoid concentration at one end of the scale, the gradient scales with the square root of the trade volume. For dense networks like this, in particular, it is very important that the edges are drawn in order of increasing relevance, otherwise the important ones may be hidden under lots of relational noise.

While size variation directs attention to the prominent actors and ties for macro-level reading, all information is still presented in context and can be inspected at the micro-level where desired.

5.4 Summary

The basic principles of network visualization are the same, irrespective of whether its purpose is the exploration of data or the presentation of findings. If a visualization helps you discover something, it is also likely to be good at conveying that something to others.

It is more important to choose the perspective from which the network is to be portrayed. Hence, we have introduced the basic elements of effective network visualization: identifying relevant types of information, and designing a graphical representation that conveys these types accurately and readably. Due to the inherent dependencies in network data and the overall complexity of graph layout, a third element involves understanding the implications of using particular layout algorithms to realize a design. There are more pitfalls in interpreting a network diagram than in many other statistical graphics.

A well-designed diagram, however, is the most powerful way of communicating the findings of a network study. The juxtaposition of multiple data dimensions facilitates the discovery of relations between them, the simultaneous representation of analytical results and their basis supports plausibility checking, and aesthetic appeal and higher-level shapes help with memorization.

More specialized aspects of visualization exist which we were unable to touch on in this chapter. These include techniques for the interactive

Box 21: Top 10 Visualization Tips

1. *Accuracy first, readability second, aesthetics third*
   There is little use in readable pictures conveying false information, and scientific illustrations need to be functional; like a grand statement, a beautiful picture is more likely to be remembered.
2. *Separate layers of information*
   e.g., by creating a foreground and a background using colors, high-lighting.
3. *Separate levels of information*
   e.g., by size variation or extra space between groups
4. *Local features for local information*
   e.g., node size for degree, position for other centralities.
5. *Shapes with matching degrees of freedom*
   e.g., if actor attributes are represented by node size, use round nodes in case of a single actor attribute, and rectangular nodes in case of two.
6. *Avoid overlap, change scale if necessary*
   It is better to have small nodes than overlapping ones if it is not clear whether they hide something.
7. *Consider previous knowledge and viewing traditions*
   e.g., many sociologists will be confused if you represent male actors with circles and female actors with triangle; break with traditions if they hinder reading.
8. *Choose balanced colors and palettes*
   Color should be distinguishable yet pleasing; it may have connotations.
9. *Explain what you did*
   Given that the available graphical variables are always the same but the information they represent usually is not, the mapping of data to graphical elements needs to be explained; as diagrams are often viewed without reading the surrounding paragraphs, use a legend or caption.
10. *Be consistent across visualizations*
    It is easier to memorize and recognize information that is mapped using repeated designs.

exploration of network data, such as semantic lenses and focus+context distortions, and techniques for other types of data, such as longitudinal networks.

We concluded with a list of guidelines (Box 21) that should help you with the purposeful production of pleasing images. Just as there is no single technique for analzying all networks, these guideliness are not universally applicable. However, they can clearly assist in facilitating more informed decision-making.

5.5 Exercises

1. Pick a network visualization program that supports both automatic and manual node placement. Draw any network of at least 42 actors using either a spring embedder layout algorithm or multidimensional scaling. Then, do the following:

   - Move nodes manually to emphasize cohesive groups.

   - Move nodes manually to increase or decrease the perceived density of cohesive groups.

   - Check which nodes in the center of the drawing are also central according to closeness and betweenness centrality.

   - Identify pairs of structurally equivalent actors and compare their positions. What about regular equivalence?

   - Try to direct a viewers attention to a selected part of the network by assigning it more display space. Rearrange the rest of the network so that it remains readable.

2. Answer the following questions from inspection of Figure 36(a)

   - Is the triad of BU, ET, and SO balanced?

   - How many directed paths connect TA to RG?

   - Do BU and HM have similar neighborhoods?

3. Pick a network visualization from the "social networks" category of the VisualComplexity.com Web site (Lima 2011) and analyze its design:

   - Which representation has been used?

- Which layout principle has been realized using which algorithm?
- Which data are mapped to which graphical variables?
- How is the design explained to the reader?
- Which elements of the visualization are particularly attractive or annoying?

What are the relations between substantive content, data, and graphical representation? Can you think of improvements?

4. Pick any network data set and explicitly write down a visualization design by tabulating data attributes and their type, specifying a representation, and so on. Try to implement this design as accurately as possible and show the result to friends or colleagues. Do they realize your intentions? Does the picture convey the desired information to them?

5. Repeat the previous task, only this time try to be (i) confusing or (ii) suggestive. For example, you may want to hide a prominent structural feature of your network or even convey the opposite; or you could try to plant fake "insights" into your diagram. Using graphical variables from the bottom half of Figure 41 may be helpful for this task.

6. Suppose you are designing a sociogram, in which you would like to represent size and density of the neighborhood of each actor (i.e., degree and clustering coefficient). What are your choices and what are their advantages and disadvantages?

7. The original diagram of the advice network in Figure 44(b) was "drawn so that the arrows tended to point upward on the page" (Krackhardt 1996: 165). Thus, informal status is defined implicitly by the (manually performed) drawing algorithm. Discuss the relation of this notion of status to the concept of status indices as defined in Section 4.2.3 and used in the drawing above.

8. Discuss the possibility of representing blockmodels in sociograms.

9. For the figures in this chapter we have made extensive use of layering based on the gestalt principle of *figure and ground*: Frontal, black graphical elements appear to be placed on top of a background of grey elements of lesser importance. Other pertinent gestalt principles are *connectedness* and *proximity*. Identify their use in this chapter and discuss potential applications of other gestalt principles in network visualization.

10. Pick a research article with a network visualization and create a legend for it. Can the figure be understood without the accompanying text? Which part of the message could not be communicated graphically? Why?

6 Summary

This textbook is organized on the basis of the research process and focuses on those aspects that are particular to network analysis in comparison with other empirical research. Because of the broad interdisciplinary use of network analysis, however, we do not cover substantive, and therefore domain-specific, network theories.

This textbook is meant to be a guide to empirical network research for a broad audience of students, researchers, and practitioners. It is based on the research process and highlights different issues that must be taken into account in the course of the research process.

However, it is important to understand that network research itself involves a network of different scientific disciplines and users, which and who influence network research in very different ways (see the historiographic account of Freeman 2004). Applications of analytical and illustrative methods have been developed in the fields of physics, mathematics, and computer science, in particular. The theories also differ on the basis of their origins which are mainly located in anthropology, psychology, and sociology. For this reason, we do not provide an account of the history of network research as it is not an essential element of the concrete research process.

The broad adoption of network perspectives is supported by a diverse variety of theoretical foundations. From our perspective, there cannot be a unifying, substantive network theory underlying all of network analysis. Hence, we do not provide a separate chapter on network theory but limit ourselves to explaining the theoretical assumptions of relevance to the different topics in association with the various examples provided.

Each domain requires its own network theories, and these may be refined to varying extents at present. For those interested in network theory, we recommend Emirbayer and Goodwin (1994), Borgatti and Halgin (2011), and Kadushin (2011) as starting points. A domain-oriented textbook is Valente (2010).

The situation with regard to analytic methodology is quite similar. In other words, network research does not involve a uniform methodological framework (Brandes and Erlebach 2005). The study of relational structures constitutes the common basis of all of the different currents. The research questions that follow a network-analytic approach are based on the fundamental understanding that what we observe in networks is not independent. This means that the focus of interest in network research is the question as to how social actors are connected with each other, and thus influence each other's behavior, and how the resulting interactions influence the entire network structure. Based on this view, it is possible to differentiate between two different types of network-analytic questions:

1. How and why actors interact with each other in an observed way;
2. What are the consequences that result from the found network structure, e.g., the performance or scope of the exchange of resources?

In the first case, the network would be the dependent variable and, in the second, it would be the explanatory variable.

Such research questions can, however, be answered from very different access points and on different levels of aggregation. Hence, network research can be undertaken from different vantage points. Attention can be focused on the individual, for example. In this case, the relationships between a focal actor and the alteri is analyzed and, perhaps also, the relationships between these alteri. Such an analysis can be qualitative, and may be carried out using network maps, for example. Alternatively, it may be quantitative in that a network generator runs along with a representative survey. The claim is that such data can explain the behavior, attitudes, and entire habitus of a person as aggregates of a class or group. With the help of such an approach, it is possible to link attributes with network insights and in this way obtain more informative data than would be possible if the research were limited to one of the two areas. The theoretical basis of such an approach can be found, for example, in Bourdieu's reflections on the reproduction of class society through the socializing appropriation of cultural and social capital with the corresponding class-specific habitus (Hennig and Kohl 2011).

Another approach involves surveying complete networks, in which case the characteristics of people play a role that is far less significant or, possibly, even negligible. The analysis then involves a network that has been circumscribed in some way, and the focus of interest is the relationship structure within this complete network. In general, the information available on such complete networks is less substantive on the level of the individual participants. However, more information is generally available about the possibilities for information flows, the group constellation, and the positions within the circumscribed frame. What is of interest here, therefore, is generally not the individual and his individual socialization. Hence, we can say that the situation is more important than the socialization here, and we obtain a completely different view of the emergence and significance of the social in this case. A theoretical basis is more likely to be found here in all of the explanations that consider situations and constellation and emergent structures. Corresponding authors on a very general level would be Simmel, Goffman, and White.

The general approach to and organization of network-analytic studies do not differ fundamentally from more traditional empirical research. The procedures used in the analysis of relational data are very similar to those used in the analyses of non-relational ones. The real difference with regard to traditional empirical social research consists in the fact that dyads are studied rather than monads. The term "social network," denoting a construct, is used here because all of the basic units of network analysis are dyads. This means that social networks consist of a large number of such dyads which are not independent of each other. Dyadic variables describe the relationship between two actors. The actors are represented by nodes within a formalized network, and their relations and effects in and on a social network are analyzed. These dyads, which are strongly dependent on each other, form a bigger structure which is described using the term "social network." This means that the concept of the social network is a relational metaphor, which is used to visualize complex structures through nodes and line segments which represent the actors and their relatedness.

The link to an underlying network theory is best established through a dyad index because this evaluates the specific quality of the relations between pairs of actors. Most methods essentially aggregate evaluations of particular dyads. Moreover, they are generic in the sense that very often one dyad index can be replaced by another one, if that is more appropriate in a specific context.

While the discussed methods of analysis are often used for description, the quantities determined through them may also be core variables for inferential statistics. In addition, we have seen that modeling a population of networks, to which observations are contrasted, is a complex task and an area that is still under development.

We have deliberately omitted longitudinal networks because the inclusion of time leads to a combinatorial explosion of cases for consideration. This is because different kinds of dynamics can be present in attributes, structure, composition, processes taking place in a network, externalities, and any combination thereof. Each of these can be present in any of the types of analyses discussed. Let us simply note that the usual first steps are time series analyses of the variable determined on the basis of cross-sectional snapshots of a longitudinal network and the actor-oriented modeling approach (Snijders et al. 2010).

Irrespective of whether its purpose is the exploration of data or presentation of findings, the principles of network visualization are the same. If a visualization helps you discover something, it is also likely to be good at conveying that "something" to others. It is more important to choose the perspective, from which the network is to be portrayed.

A well-designed diagram, however, is the most powerful way of communicating the findings of a network study. The juxtaposition of multiple data dimensions facilitates the discovery of relations between them, the simultaneous representation of analytical results and their basis supports plausibility checking, and the aesthetic appeal and higher-level shapes help with memorizing. More specialized aspects also exist that we did not touch on. These include techniques for the interactive exploration of network data, such as semantic lenses and focus plus context distortions, and techniques for other types of data, such as longitudinal networks.

Social networks can be surveyed, visualized, and analyzed with the help of computer programs. The standard programs for the statistical analysis of social scientific data are limited in their suitability for network analysis. Although tried-and-tested statistical software packages can be used for ego-centered network analysis, they are not suited to the analysis of complete networks. An extensive overview of software tools available for collection, analysis, and visualization of network data is maintained on Wikipedia.[1] Most of these tools can be used to carry out both ego-centered analysis and complete network analyses.

---

1 http://en.wikipedia.org/wiki/Social_network_analysis_software

The most that this book can achieve is to inspire you to go on with network research. Hence, we would like to take the opportunity to draw your attention to INSNA (`www.insna.org`), the professional association for researchers interested in social network analysis. The network was founded by Barry Wellman in 1978 and involves researchers from all over the world. Its members collaborate on questions concerning network theory, methodology, analysis, visualization, and software development. The network meets annually at the Sunbelt Social Network Conference to report on the latest research and promote cooperative ventures—in fact, this book was initiated at such a meeting. INSNA also publishes a quarterly journal, *Connections*, and there are three journals that focus exclusively on network-related research, *Social Networks*, the *Journal of Social Structure*, and *Network Science*.

List of Figures

List of Boxes

About the Authors

Marina Hennig is Professor for Social Network Research and Sociology of the Family at Johannes Gutenberg-University Mainz. She studied sociology at Humboldt Universität zu Berlin. She was awarded her doctorate in 1999 and *venia legendi* in 2006, both by Humboldt Universität. Her post-doctoral thesis was about individuals and their social relations and her research focuses on ego-centered network analysis, family ties in contemporary urban Germany, the generation of social capital in online social networks, and the further substantiation of the network perspective. Her most recent research project (2009–2011) focused on an empirical reconstruction of the Pierre Bourdieu's habitus-field theory of using network analysis.

Ulrik Brandes has been Professor for Algorithmics at the University of Konstanz since 2003. He studied computer science at RWTH Aachen and received his doctorate degree and *venia legendi* in computer science from the University of Konstanz in 1999 and 2002, respectively. His research interests include network analysis, graph algorithms, experimental algorithmics, graph drawing, and information visualization. He has been a member of the Board of Directors of the International Network for Social Networks Analysis (INSNA) since 2008.

Jürgen Pfeffer earned a PhD in Business Informatics from Vienna University of Technology, Austria. He worked in industry and non-university research institutes for ten years and is currently a postdoctoral associate at the School of Computer Science at Carnegie Mellon University. Jürgen Pfeffer's research combines traditional network analysis and dynamic network analysis theories and methods with up-to-date science from the areas of visual analytics, geographic information systems, system dynamics, and data mining. His research focus lies in the computational analysis of organizations and societies with a special emphasis on dynamics and change in large-scale systems.

Ines Mergel is Assistant Professor of Public Administration and International Affairs at the Maxwell School of Citizenship and Public Affairs, Syracuse University, NY. She studied business administration at the University of Kassel, Germany, and the Reijksuniversiteit Leiden, The Netherlands. She was awarded a doctorate in business administration by the University of St. Gallen, Switzerland, in 2005 and spent six years as a research fellow at the Program on Networked Governance at Harvard Kennedy School of Government, Cambridge, MA. Her research focuses on the diffusion and adoption of social media applications among public managers in the U.S. federal government. She is the author of *Social Media in the Public Sector: A Guide to Participation, Collaboration and Transparency in The Networked World* (2012) and co-authored the companion field guide (2012, with Bill Greeves). Her research has been published in leading public administration journals.

Bibliography

Allison, P. D. (2001). *Missing Data*, Volume 07-136 of *Sage University Papers Series on Quantitative Applications in the Social Sciences*. Thousand Oaks, CA: Sage.

Axelrod, R. M. (1997). *The Complexity of Cooperation: Agent-Based Models of Competition and Collaboration*. Princeton, NJ: Princeton University Press.

Babbie, E. R. (2009). *The Practice of Social Research* (12th ed.). Belmont, CA: Wadsworth.

Baker, D. R. (1992). A structural analysis of the social work journal network: 1985-196. *Journal of Social Service Research 15* (3-4), 153-168.

Bakshy, E., I. Rosenn, C. Marlow, and L. Adamic (2012). The role of social networks in information diffusion. In *Proceedings of the 21st International World Wide Web Conference (WWW2012)*, 519-528. ACM Press.

Barabási, A.-L. and R. Albert (1999). Emergence of scaling in random networks. *Science 286*, 509-512.

Barnes, J. A. (1954). Class and committees in a Norwegian island parish. *Human Relations 7*, 39-58.

Barnes, J. A. (1972). Social networks. *Addison-Wesley Module in Anthropology 26*, 1-29.

Barnes, J. A. (1979). Network analysis: orienting notion, rigorous technique or substantive filed of study. In P. W. Holland and S. Leinhardt (Eds.), *Perspectives on Social Network Research*, 403-433. New York, NY: Academic Press.

Bavelas, A. (1950). Communication patterns in task-oriented groups. *Journal of the Acoustical Society of America 22* (6), 725-730.

Bearman, P. S., J. Moody, and K. Stovel (2004). Chains of affection: The structure of adolescent romantic and sexual networks. *American Journal of Sociology 110*, 44-91.

Bernard, H. R. (2011). *Research Methods in Anthropology: Qualitative and Quantitative Approaches* (5th ed.). Lanham, MD: Altamira.

Bernard, H. R. (2012). *Social Research Methods: Qualitative and Quantitative Approaches*. Thousand Oaks, CA: Sage.

Bernard, H. R., E. C. Johnson, P. D. Killworth, D. Kronenfeld, and L. Sailer (1985). On the validity on retrospective data: The problem of the informant accuracy. *Annual Review of Anthropology 13*, 495–517.

Bernard, H. R., P. D. Killworth, and L. Sailer (1980). Informant accuracy in social network data IV. *Social Networks 2*, 191–218.

Bernard, H. R., P. D. Killworth, and L. Sailer (1982). Informant accuracy in social network data V: An experimental attempt to predict actual communication from recall data. *Social Science Research 11*, 30–66.

Bertin, J. (1983). *Semiology of Graphics: Diagrams, Networks, Maps*. Madison, WI: University of Wisconsin Press.

Blau, P. M. (1977). *Inequality and Heterogeneity: A Primitive Theory of Social Structure*. New York, NY: The Free Press.

Bollobás, B. (2001). *Random Graphs* (2nd ed.). Cambridge, UK: Cambridge University Press.

Bonacich, P. (1972). Factoring and weighting approaches to status scores and clique identification. *Journal of Mathematical Sociology 2*, 113–120.

Bonacich, P. (1987). Power and centrality: A family of measures. *American Journal of Sociology 92* (5), 1170–1182.

Bonacich, P. and P. Lloyd (2001). Eigenvector-like measures of centrality for asymmetric relations. *Social Networks 23* (3), 191–201.

Borgatti, S. P. (1997). Unpacking Burt's redundancy measures. *Connections 20* (1), 35–38.

Borgatti, S. P. (2005). Centrality and network flow. *Social Networks 27* (1), 55–71.

Borgatti, S. P. (2009). 2-mode concepts in social network analysis. In R. A. Meyers (Ed.), *Encyclopedia of Complexity and System Science*, 8279–8291. New York, NY: Springer-Verlag.

Borgatti, S. P. and M. G. Everett (1997). Network analysis of 2-mode data. *Social Networks 19* (3), 243–269.

Borgatti, S. P. and M. G. Everett (1999). Models of core/periphery structures. *Social Networks 21* (4), 375–395.

Borgatti, S. P. and M. G. Everett (2006). A graph-theoretic framework for classifying centrality measures. *Social Networks 28* (4), 466–484.

Borgatti, S. P., M. G. Everett, and P. R. Shirey (1990). LS sets, lambda sets and other cohesive subsets. *Social Networks 12* (4), 337–357.

Borgatti, S. P. and D. S. Halgin (2011). On network theory. *Organization Science 22* (5), 1359–1367.

Borgatti, S. P., A. Mehra, D. J. Brass, and G. Labianca (2009). Network analysis in the social sciences. *Science 323* (5916), 892–895.

Borgatti, S. P. and J. L. Molina (2003). Ethical and strategic issues in organizational social network analysis. *Journal of Applied Behavioral Science 39* (3), 337–349.

Borgatti, S. P. and J. L. Molina (2005). Toward ethical guidelines for network research in organizations. *Social Networks 27* (2), 107–117.

Bott, E. (1964). *Family and social network: roles, norms and external relationship in ordinary urban families.* London, UK: Tavistock.

Bourdieu, P. (1983). Ökonomisches Kapital, kulturelles Kapital, soziales Kapital. In R. Kreckel (Ed.), *Soziale Ungleichheiten,* 183–198. Göttingen, Germany: Otto Schwartz.

Brandes, U. (2001). Drawing on physical analogies. In M. Kaufmann and D. Wagner (Eds.), *Drawing Graphs: Methods and Models,* Volume 2025 of *Lecture Notes in Computer Science,* 71–86. Springer-Verlag.

Brandes, U., D. Delling, M. Gaertler, R. Görke, M. Hoefer, Z. Nikoloski, and D. Wagner (2008). On modularity clustering. *IEEE Transactions on Knowledge and Data Engineering 20* (2), 172–188.

Brandes, U. and T. Erlebach (Eds.) (2005). *Network Analysis: Methodological Foundations,* Volume 3418 of *Lecture Notes in Computer Science.* Berlin, Germany: Springer-Verlag.

Brandes, U., P. Kenis, J. Raab, V. Schneider, and D. Wagner (1999). Explorations into the visualization of policy networks. *Journal of Theoretical Politics 11* (1), 75–106.

Brandes, U., J. Lerner, M. J. Lubbers, C. McCarty, and J. L. Molina (2008). Visual statistics for collections of clustered graphs. In *Proceedings of the IEEE Pacific Visualization Symposium (PacificVis'08),* 47–54. IEEE Computer Society Press.

Brandes, U. and B. Nick (2011). Asymmetric relations in longitudinal social networks. *IEEE Transactions on Visualization and Computer Graphics 17* (12), 2283–2290.

Brandes, U. and C. Pich (2009). An experimental study on distance-based graph drawing. In *Proceedings of the 16th International Symposium on Graph Drawing (GD'08),* Volume 5417 of *Lecture Notes in Computer Science,* 218–229. Springer-Verlag.

Brandes, U. and V. Schneider (2009). Netzwerkbilder: Politiknetzwerke in Metaphern, Modellen und Visualisierungen. In V. Schneider,

F. Janning, P. Leifeld, and T. Malang (Eds.), *Politiknetzwerke. Modelle, Anwendungen und Visualisierungen*, 31–58. Wiesbaden, Germany: VS Verlag für Sozialwissenschaften.

Breiger, R. L. (2005). Introduction to special issue: ethical dilemmas in social network research. *Social Networks 27* (2), 89–93.

Breiger, R. L., S. A. Boorman, and P. Arabie (1975). An algorithm for clustering relational data with applications to soci al network analysis and comparison with multidimensional scaling. *Journal of Mathematical Psychology 12*, 328–383.

Breiger, R. L. and P. E. Pattison (1986). Cumulated social roles: The duality of persons and their algebras. *Social Networks 8* (3), 215–256.

Brin, S. and L. Page (1998). The anatomy of a large-scale hypertextual Web search engine. *Computer Networks and ISDN Systems 30* (1–7), 107–117.

Burt, R. S. (1983). *Corporate Profits and Cooptation: Networks of Market Constraints and Directorate Ties in the American Economy*. New York, NY: Academic Press.

Burt, R. S. (1984). Network items and the general social survey. *Social Networks 6* (4), 293–339.

Burt, R. S. (1992). *Structural Holes*. Cambridge, MA: Harvard University Press.

Burt, R. S. (2004). Structural holes and good ideas. *American Journal of Sociology 110*, 349–399.

Butts, C. T. (2003). Network inference, error, and informant (in)accuracy: a Bayesian approach. *Social Networks 25* (2), 103–140.

Butts, C. T. (2009). Revisiting the foundations of network analysis. *Science 325* (5939), 414–416.

Carley, K. M. (1999). On the evolution of social organizational networks. In S. B. Andrews and D. Knoke (Eds.), *Research in the Sociology of Organizations*, Volume 16: Networks in and around Organizations, 3–30. Stamford, CT: JAI Press.

Carley, K. M. (2002). Smart agents and organizations of the future. In L. Lievrouw and S. Livingstone (Eds.), *The Handbook of New Media*, 206–220. Thousand Oaks, CA: Sage.

Cartwright, D. and F. Harary (1956). Structural balance: A generalization of Heider's theory. *Psychological Review 63*, 277–93.

Cooper, J. N. and L. Lu (2007). Where do power laws come from? arXiv:math/0702463v1 [math.CO].

Davis, A., B. B. Gardner, and M. R. Gardner (1941). *Deep South: A Social Anthropological Study of Caste and Class*. Chicago, IL: University of Chicago Press.

Davis, J. A. (1963). Structural balance, mechanical solidarity and interpersonal relations. *American Journal of Sociology 68*, 444–461.

De Benedictis, L. and L. Tajoli (2011). The world trade network. *The World Economy 34* (8), 1417–1454.

Dekker, D., D. Krackhardt, and T. A. Snijders (2007). Sensitivity of MRQAP tests to collinearity and autocorrelation conditions. *Psychometrika 72* (4), 563–581.

Diaz-Bone, R. (1997). *Ego-zentrierte Netzwerkanalyse und familiale Beziehungssysteme*. Wiesbaden, Germany: Deutscher Universitätsverlag.

Doreian, P., V. Batagelj, and A. Ferligoj (2004). Generalized blockmodeling of two-mode network data. *Social Networks 26* (1), 29–53. Corrigendum in 26(4):349, 2004.

Doreian, P., V. Batagelj, and A. Ferligoj (2005). *Generalized Blockmodeling*. Cambridge, UK: Cambridge University Press.

Eades, P. (1984). A heuristic for graph drawing. *Congressus Numerantium 42*, 149–160.

Eklund, P., J. Ducrou, and P. Brawn (2004). Concept lattices for information visualization: Can novices read line-diagrams? In *Proceedings of the 2nd International Conference on Formal Concept Analysis (ICFCA'04)*, Volume 2961 of *Lecture Notes in Computer Science*, 235–236. Springer-Verlag.

Emirbayer, M. and J. Goodwin (1994). Network analysis, culture, and the problem of agency. *American Journal of Sociology 99* (6), 1411–1454.

Everett, M. G. and S. P. Borgatti (1994). Regular equivalence: General theory. *Journal of Mathematical Sociology 18* (1), 29–52.

Everett, M. G. and S. P. Borgatti (1996). Exact colorations of graphs and digraphs. *Social Networks 18* (4), 319–331.

Everett, M. G. and D. Krackhardt (2012). A second look at Krackhardt's graph theoretical dimensions of informal organizations. *Social Networks 34* (2), 159–163.

Faust, K. (1997). Centrality in affiliation networks. *Social Networks 19* (2), 157–191.

Festinger, L. (1957). *A Theory of Cognitive Dissonance*. Evanston, IL: Row, Preston & Co.

Fischer, C. S. (1982). *To Dwell Among Friends. Personal Networks in Town and City*. Chicago, IL: University of Chicago Press.

Flap, H. (2002). No man is an island. In O. Favereau and E. Lazega (Eds.), *Conventions and Structures in Economic Organization. Markets, Networks and Hierarchies*, 29–59. London, UK: Edward Elgar.

Forsyth, E. and L. Katz (1946). A matrix approach to the analysis of sociometric data: Preliminary report. *Sociometry 9*, 340–347.

Fortunato, S. (2010). Community detection in graphs. *Physics Reports 486* (3–5), 75–174.

Fowler, Jr., F. J. (2009). *Survey Research Methods* (4th ed.). Thousand Oaks, CA: Sage.

France, S. L. and J. D. Carroll (2011). Two-way multidimensional scaling: a review. *IEEE Transactions on Systems, Man, and Cybernetics—Part C: Applications and Reviews 41* (5), 644–661.

Freeman, L. C. (1977). A set of measures of centrality based on betweenness. *Sociometry 40* (1), 35–41.

Freeman, L. C. (1979). Centrality in social networks: Conceptual clarification. *Social Networks 1* (3), 215–239.

Freeman, L. C. (1989). Social networks and the structure experiment. In L. C. Freeman, D. R. White, and A. K. Romney (Eds.), *Research Methods in Social Network Analysis*, 11–40. New Brunswick, NJ: Transaction Publishers.

Freeman, L. C. (2003). Finding social groups: A meta-analysis of the southern women data. In R. L. Breiger, K. M. Carley, and P. E. Pattison (Eds.), *Dynamic Social Network Modeling and Analysis*. Washington, DC: The National Academies Press.

Freeman, L. C. (2004). *The Development of Social Network Analysis: A Study in the Sociology of Science*. Vancouver, BC: Empirical Press.

Freeman, L. C. and A. K. Romney (1987). Words, deeds and social structure: A preliminiary study of the reliabibilty of informants. *Human Organizations 46*, 330–334.

Freeman, L. C., A. K. Romney, and S. C. Freeman (1987). Cognitive structure and informant accuracy. *American Anthropologist 89*, 310–325.

Freeman, L. C. and D. R. White (1993). Using galois lattices to represent network data. *Sociological Methodology 23*, 127–146.

Fried, M. (1963). Grieving for a lost home. In L. J. Duhl (Ed.), *The Urban Condition: People and Policy in the Metropolis*, 151–171. New York, NY: Basic Books.

Fruchterman, T. M. J. and E. M. Reingold (1991). Graph drawing by force-directed placement. *Software - Practice and Experience 21* (11), 1129–1164.

Gans, H. J. (1962). *The urban villagers: group and class in the life of Italian-Americans, Reprint edition.* New York, NY: The Free Press.

Ghoniem, M., J.-D. Fekete, and P. Castagliola (2005). On the readability of graphs using node-link and matrix-based representations: a controlled experiment and statistical analysis. *Information Visualization 4* (2), 114–135.

Glynn, T. J. (1981). Psychological sense of community: Measurement and application. *Human Relations 34*, 780–818.

Goldenberg, A., A. X. Zheng, S. E. Fienberg, and E. M. Airoldi (2009). A survey of statistical network models. *Foundations and Trends in Machine Learning 2* (2), 129–233.

Good, B. H., Y.-A. de Montjoye, and A. Clauset (2010). Performance of modularity maximization in practical contexts. *Physical Review E 81* (4), 046106.

Goodreau, S. M., J. A. Kitts, and M. Morris (2009). Birds of a feather or friends of a friend? using exponential random graph models to investigate adolescent social networks. *Demography 46* (1), 103–125.

Gower, J. C. (1966). Some distance properties of latent root and vector methods used in multivariate analysis. *Biometrika 53*, 325–338.

Granovetter, M. S. (1973). The strength of weak ties. *American Journal of Sociology 78* (6), 1360–1380.

Granovetter, M. S. (1974). *Getting a job.* Chicago, IL: University of Chicago Press.

Granovetter, M. S. (1985). Economic action and social structure: The problem of embeddedness. *American Journal of Sociology 91*, 481–510.

Greer, S. (1962). *The Emerging City.* New York, NY: The Free Press.

Hammer, M. (1985). Implications of behavioral and cognitive reciprocity in social network data. *Social Networks 7* (2), 189–201.

Heider, F. (1946). Attitudes and cognitive organizations. *Journal of Psychology 21*, 107–112.

Heidler, R. (2008). Zur Evolution sozialer Netzwerke. Theoretische Implikationen einer akteursbasierten Methode in: Netzwerkanalyse und Netzwerktheorie. In C. Stegbauer (Ed.), *Eine neues Paradigma in den Sozialwissenschaften*, 359–372. Wiesbaden, Germany: VS Verlag für Sozialwissenschaften.

Hennig, M. and S. Kohl (2011). *Rahmen und Spielräume sozialer Beziehungen. Zum Einfluss des Habitus auf die Herausbildung von Netzwerkstrukturen*. Netzwerkforschung. Wiesbaden, Germany: VS Verlag für Sozialwissenschaften.

Henry, N., J.-D. Fekete, and M. J. McGuffin (2007). NodeTrix: a hybrid visualization of social networks. *IEEE Transactions on Visualization and Computer Graphics 13* (6), 1302–1309.

Hill, S., F. Provost, and C. Volinsky (2006). Network-based marketing: Identifying likely adopters via consumer networks. *Statistical Science 21* (2), 256–276.

Holland, P. W. and S. Leinhardt (1970). A method for detecting structure in sociometric data. *American Journal of Sociology 76* (3), 492–513.

Holland, P. W. and S. Leinhardt (1976). The statistical analysis of local structure in social networks. In D. R. Heise (Ed.), *Sociological Methodology*, 1–45. San Francisco, CA: Jossey-Bass.

Huberman, B. A., D. M. Romero, and F. Wu (2009). Social networks that matter: Twitter under the microscope. *First Monday 14* (1–5).

Hunter, D. R. and M. S. Handcock (2006). Inference in curved exponential family models for networks. *Journal of Computational and Graphical Statistics 15* (3), 565–583.

Jacobs, J. (1961). *The Death and Life of Great American Cities*. New York, NY: Random House.

Joshi, A. (2006). The influence of organizational demography on the external networking behavior of teams. *Academy of Management Review 31* (3), 583–595.

Kadushin, C. (2005). Who benefits from network analysis: Ethics of social network research. *Social Networks 27* (2), 139–153.

Kadushin, C. (2011). *Understanding Social Networks: Theories, Concepts, and Findings*. New York, NY: Oxford University Press.

Kahn, R. L. and T. C. Antonucci (1980). *Social Networks in Adult Life. Network Questionnaire*. Dearborn, MI: University of Michigan.

Katz, L. (1947). On the matric analysis of sociometric data. *Sociometry 10*, 233–241.

Katz, L. (1953). A new status index derived from sociometric analysis. *Psychometrika 18* (1), 39–43.

Kenny, D. A., D. A. Kashy, and W. L. Cook (2006). *Dyadic Data Analysis*. New York, NY: Guilford Press.

Klovdahl, A. S. (2005). Social network research and human subjects protection: Towards more effective infectious disease control. *Social Networks 27* (2), 119–137.

Knecht, A. B. (2008). *Friendship Selection and Friends' Influence*. Ph. D. thesis, Universiteit Utrecht.

Knoke, D. and J. H. Kuklinski (1982). *Network analysis: Quantitative applications in social sciences*. Thousand Oaks, CA: Sage.

Kochen, M. (Ed.) (1989). *The Small World: A Volume of Recent Research Advances Commemorating Ithiel de Sola Pool, Stanley Milgram, Theodore Newcomb*. Norwood, NJ: Ablex Publishing Corp.

Kossinets, G. (2006). Effects of missing data in social networks. *Social Networks 28* (3), 247–268.

Krackhardt, D. (1987). QAP partialling as a test of spuriousness. *Social Networks 9*, 171–186.

Krackhardt, D. (1994). Graph theoretical dimensions of informal organization. In K. M. Carley and M. Prietula (Eds.), *Computational Organizational Theory*, 89–111. Hillsdale, NJ: Lawrence Erlbaum Associates.

Krackhardt, D. (1996). Social networks and the liability of newness for managers. In C. L. Cooper and D. M. Rousseau (Eds.), *Trends in Organizational Behavior*, Volume 3, 159–173. New York, NY: Wiley.

Krackhardt, D. (1999). The ties that torture: Simmelian tie analysis in organizations. In S. B. Andrews and D. Knoke (Eds.), *Research in the Sociology of Organizations*, Volume 16: Networks in and around Organizations, 183–210. Stamford, CT: JAI Press.

Kruskal, J. B. (1964). Multidimensional scaling for optimizing goodness of fit to a nonmetric hypothesis. *Psychometrika 29* (1), 1–27.

Kruskal, J. B. and J. B. Seery (1980). Designing network diagrams. In *Proceedings 1st General Conference on Social Graphics*, Washington, D.C., 22–50. U.S. Department of the Census.

Laidler, H. W. (1931). *Concentration of Control in American Industry*. New York, NY: Crowell Publications.

Laumann, E. O., P. V. Marsden, and D. Prensky (1989). The boundary specification problem in social network analysis. In L. C. Freeman, D. R. White, and A. K. Romney (Eds.), *Research Methods in Social Network Analysis*, 61–87. New Brunswick, NJ: Transaction Publishers.

Lazarsfeld, P. F. and R. K. Merton (1954). Friendship as a social process: A substantive and methodological analysis. In M. Berger, T. Abel, and C. H. Page (Eds.), *In Freedom and control in modern society*, 18–66. New York, NY: Van Nostrand.

Li, L., D. Alderson, J. C. Doyle, and W. Willinger (2005). Towards a theory of scale-free graphs: Definition, properties, and implications. *Internet Mathematics 2* (4), 431–523.

Liben-Nowell, D. and J. M. Kleinberg (2007). The link-prediction problem for social networks. *Journal of the American Society for Information Science and Technology 58* (7), 1019–1031.

Lima, M. (2011). *Visual Complexity: Mapping Patterns of Information.* New York, NY: Princeton Architectural Press.

Lin, N. (2001). *Social Capital: A Theory of Social Structure and Action.* Cambridge, UK: Cambridge University Press.

Lin, N. and M. Dumin (1986). Access to occupations through social ties. *Social Networks 8*, 365–385.

Lin, N., Y.-C. Fu, and R.-M. Hsung (2001). The position generator: Measurement techniques for investigation of social capital. In N. Lin, K. S. Cook, and R. S. Burt (Eds.), *Social Capital. Theory and Research*, 57–81. New Brunswick, NJ: Transaction Publishers.

Little, R. J. A. and D. B. Rubin (1989). The analysis of social science data with missing values. *Sociological Methods and Research 18* (2), 292–326.

Little, R. J. A. and N. Schenker (1995). Missing data. In G. Arminger, C. C. Clogg, and M. E. Sobel (Eds.), *Handbook of Statistical Modeling for the Social and Behavioral Sciences.* New York, NY: Plenum Press.

Lohr, S. L. (2009). *Sampling: Design and Analysis* (2nd ed.). Boston, MA: Duxbury Press.

Lorrain, F. and H. C. White (1971). Structural equivalence of individuals in social networks. *Journal of Mathematical Sociology 1* (1), 49–80.

Luce, R. D. and A. Perry (1949). A method of matrix analysis of group structure. *Psychometrika 14*, 95–116.

Luczkovich, J. J., S. P. Borgatti, J. C. Johnson, and M. G. Everett (2003). Defining and measuring trophic role similarity in food webs using regular equivalence. *Journal of Theoretical Biology 220*, 303–321.

Lundberg, G. A. and M. Lawsing (1937). The sociography of some community relations. *American Sociological Review 2*, 318–335.

Lundberg, G. A. and M. Steele (1938). Social attraction-patterns in a village. *Sociometry 1*, 375–419.

Mackinlay, J. (1986). Automating the design of graphical presentations of relational information. *ACM Transactions on Graphics 5* (2), 110–141.

Marsden, P. V. (1987). Core discussion networks of americans. *American Sociological Review 52*, 122–131.

Marsden, P. V. (2005). Recent developments in network measurement. In P. J. Carrington, J. Scott, and S. Wasserman (Eds.), *Models and Methods Social Network Analysis*, 8–30. New York, NY: Cambridge University Press.

McCallister, L. and C. S. Fischer (1978). Procedure for surveying personal networks. *Sociological Methods and Research 7*, 131–148.

McCurdy, D. W., J. P. Spradley, and D. J. Shandy (2005). *The Cultural Experience: Ethnography in Complex Society*. Long Grove, IL: Waveland Press.

McPherson, M., L. Smith-Lovin, and J. M. Cook (2001). Birds of a feather: Homophily in social networks. *Annual Review of Sociology 27*, 415–444.

Merton, R. K. (1968). The Matthew effect in science. *Science 159* (3810), 56–63.

Milgram, S. (1967). The small world problem. *Psychology Today 5*, 60–67.

Mintz, B. A. and M. Schwartz (1985). *The Power Structure of American Business*. Chicago, IL: University of Chicago Press.

Mizruchi, M. S. and C. Marquis (2006). Egocentric, sociocentric, or dyadic? Identifying the appropriate level of analysis in the study of organizational networks. *Social Networks 28* (3), 187–208.

Molina, J. L., J. Lerner, and S. G. Mestres (2008). Patrones de cambio de las redes personales de inmigrantes en Cataluña. *REDES – Revista hispana para el análisis de redes sociales 15* (4), 50–63.

Moreno, J. L. (1934). *Who Shall Survive? A New Approach to the Problem of Human Interrelations*. Washington, DC: Nervous and Mental Disease Publishing Co.

Moreno, J. L. (1946). Sociogram and sociomatrix: a note to the paper by Forsyth and Katz. *Sociometry 9*, 348–349.

Moreno, J. L. (1953). *Who Shall Survive? Foundations of Sociometry, Group Psychotherapy and Sociodrama*. New York, NY: Beacon House. First published in 1934.

Moreno, J. L. (1967). *Die Grundlagen der Soziometrie. Wege zur Neuordnung der Gesellschaft*. Köln/Opladen, Germany: Westdeutscher Verlag.

Moreno, J. L. (1995). *Auszüge aus der Autobiographie*. München, Germany: inScenario.

Mühlich, E., H. Zinn, W. Kröning, and I. Mühlich-Klinger (1978). Zusammenhang von gebauter Umwelt und sozialem Verhalten im

Wohn- und Wohnumweltbereich. *Schriftenreihe Städtebauliche Forschung 03.062.*

Münzel, M. (2006). *Die jüdischen Mitglieder der deutschen Wirtschaftselite 1927-1955.* Paderborn, Germany: Verlag Ferdinand Schöningh.

Nadel, S. F. (1957). *The Theory of Social Structure.* London, UK: Cohen & West.

Newcomb, T. M. (1953). An approach to the study of communicative acts. *Psychological Review 60,* 393–404.

Newcomb, T. M. (1961). *The Acquaintance Process.* New York, NY: Holt, Rinehart, and Winston.

Newman, M. E. J. and M. Girvan (2004). Finding and evaluating community structure in networks. *Physical Review E 69,* 026113.

Nordlie, P. G. (1958). *A longitudinal study of interpersonal attraction in a natural group setting.* Ph. D. thesis, Department of Psychology, University of Michigan.

Padgett, J. F. and C. K. Ansell (1993). Robust action and the rise of the medici 1400-1434. *American Journal of Sociology 98* (6), 1259–1319.

Petrie, W. M. F. (1899). Sequences in prehistoric remains. *The Journal of the Anthropological Institute of Great Britain and Ireland 29* (3/4), 295–301.

Pfenning, U. (1995). *Soziale Netzwerke in der Forschungspraxis: Zur theoretischen Perspektive, Vergleichbarkeit und Standardisierung von Erhebungsverfahren sozialer Netzwerke.* Darmstadt, Germany: Dissertations Druck Darmstadt GmbH.

Powell, W. W., D. R. White, K. W. Koput, and K. W. Koput (2005). Network dynamics and field evolution: The growth of interorganizational collaboration in the life sciences. *American Journal of Sociology 110,* 1132–1205.

Price, D. J. d. S. (1976). A general theory of bibliometric and other cumulative advantage processes. *Journal of the American Society for Information Sciences 27,* 292–306.

Radcliffe-Brown, A. R. (1940). On social structure. *The Journal of the Anthropological Institute of Great Britain and Ireland 70* (1), 1–12.

Radcliffe-Brown, A. R. (1957). *A Natural Science of Society.* Chicago, IL: University of Chicago Press.

Rapoport, A. and W. J. Horvath (1961). A study of a large sociogram. *Behavioral Science 6* (4), 279–291.

Resnick, M. D., P. S. Bearman, R. W. Blum, K. E. Bauman, K. M. Harris, J. Jones, J. Tabor, T. Beuhring, R. E. Sieving, M. Shew, M. Ireland,

L. H. Bearinger, and J. R. Udry (1997). Protecting adolescents from harm. Findings from the National Longitudinal Study on Adolescent Health. *Journal of the American Medial Association 278* (10), 823–832.

Robins, G., P. E. Pattison, Y. Kalish, and D. Lusher (2007). An introduction to exponential random graph (p^*) models for social networks. *Social Networks 29* (2), 173–191.

Robins, G., P. E. Pattison, and J. Woolcock (2004). Missing data in networks: exponential random graph (p^*) models for networks with non-respondents. *Social Networks 26*, 257–283.

Robinson, W. S. (1951). A method for chronologically ordering archaeological deposits. *American Antiquity 16* (4), 293–301.

Roethlisberger, F. J. and W. J. Dickson (1939). *Management and the Worker*. Cambridge, MA: Harvard University Press.

Rose, A. K. (2004). Do we really know that the WTO increases trade? *American Economic Review 94* (1), 98–114.

Rosenthal, N., M. Fingrudt, M. Ethier, R. Karant, and D. McDonald (1985). Social movements and network analysis: a case study of nineteenth-century women's reform in New York State. *American Journal of Sociology 90*, 1022–54.

Sabidussi, G. (1966). The centrality index of a graph. *Psychometrika 31* (4), 581–603.

Sarason, S. B. (1974). *The psychological sense of community: Prospects for a community psychology*. San Francisco, CA: Jossey-Bass.

Schaeffer, S. E. (2007). Graph clustering. *Computer Science Review 1* (1), 27–64.

Schnegg, M. (2007). Blurred edges, open boundaries: The long term development of the closed corporate peasant community in rural Mexico. *Journal of Anthropological Research 63*, 5–32.

Schweizer, T. (1996). *Muster sozialer Ordnung. Netzwerkanaylse als Fundament der Sozialethnologie*. Berlin, Germany: Dietrich Reimer Verlag.

Scott, J. (2000). *Social Network Analysis: A Handbook* (2nd ed.). London, UK: Sage.

Seidman, S. B. (1983). Network structure and minimum degree. *Social Networks 5*, 269–287.

Shepard, R. N. (1962). Analysis of proximities: Multidimensional scaling with an unknown distance function. *Psychometrika 27* (2), 125–140 and 219–246.

Sneath, P. H. A. and R. R. Sokal (1973). *Numerical Taxonomy: The*

Principles and Practice of Numerical Classification. San Francisco, CA: W. H. Freeman and Company.

Snijders, T. A. (2011). Statistical models for social networks. *Annual Review of Sociology 37*, 131–153.

Snijders, T. A. and K. Nowicki (1997). Estimation and prediction of stochastic blockmodels for graphs with latent block structure. *Journal of Classification 14*, 75–100.

Snijders, T. A., G. G. van de Bunt, and C. E. Steglich (2010). Introduction to actor-based models for network dynamics. *Social Networks 32* (1), 44–60.

Stegbauer, C. (2010). Reziprozität. In C. Stegbauer and R. Häußling (Eds.), *Handbuch der Netzwerkforschung*, 113–122. Wiesbaden, Germany: VS Verlag für Sozialwissenschaften.

Steglich, C. E. and A. B. Knecht (2010). Die statistische Analyse dynamischer Netzwerkdaten. In C. Stegbauer and R. Häußling (Eds.), *Handbuch der Netzwerkforschung*, 433–446. Wiesbaden, Germany: VS Verlag für Sozialwissenschaften.

Steglich, C. E., T. A. Snijders, and M. Pearson (2010). Dynamic networks and behavior: Separating selection from influence. *Sociological Methodology 40* (1), 329–393.

Subramanian, A. and S.-J. Wei (2007). The WTO promotes trade, strongly but unevenly. *Journal of International Economics 72*, 151–175.

Torgerson, W. S. (1952). Multidimensional scaling: I. Theory and method. *Psychometrika 17* (4), 401–419.

Trappmann, M., H.-J. Hummell, and W. Sodeur (2005). *Strukturanalyse sozialer Netzwerke. Konzepte, Modelle, Methoden*. Wiesbaden, Germany: VS Verlag für Sozialwissenschaften.

Tsai, W. (2001). Knowledge transfer in intraorganizational networks: Effects of network position and absorptive capacity on business unit innovation and performance. *Academy Of Management Journal 44* (5), 996–1004.

Tsai, W. and S. Ghoshal (1998). Social capital and value creation: The role of intrafirm networks. *Academy Of Management Journal 41* (4), 464–476.

Tufte, E. R. (1983). *The Visual Display of Quantitative Information*. Cheshire, CT: Graphics Press.

Tufte, E. R. (1990). *Envisioning Information*. Cheshire, CT: Graphics Press.

Valente, T. W. (2010). *Social Networks and Health: Models, Methods, and Applications*. New York, NY: Oxford University Press.

van der Gaag, M. and T. A. Snijders (2005). Ressoure generator: measurement of individual social capital with concrete items. *Social Networks 27*, 1–29.

Wasserman, S. and K. Faust (1994). *Social Network Aanalysis. Methods and Applications*. Cambridge, UK: Cambridge University Press.

Watts, D. J. and S. H. Strogatz (1998). Collective dynamics of 'small world' networks. *Nature 393*, 440–442.

Wellman, B. (1979). The community question: The intimate networks of East Yorkers. *American Journal of Sociology 84*, 1201–1231.

Wellman, B. (1993). An egocentric network tale. *Social Networks 15*, 423–36.

Wellman, B. and S. D. Berkowitz (Eds.) (1988). *Social Structures: A Network Approach*. New York, NY: Cambridge University Press.

Wellman, B., P. J. Carrington, and A. Hall (1988). Networks as personal communities. See Wellman and Berkowitz (1988), 130–185.

Wellman, B., P. Carven, M. Whitaker, H. Stevens, A. Shorter, S. DuTroit, and H. Bakker (1973). Community ties and support systems: From intimacy to support. In L. S. Bourne, R. D. MacKinnon, and J. W. Simmons (Eds.), *The Form of Cities in Central Canada*. Toronto, Canada: University of Toronto Press.

Wellman, B. and R. Hiscott (1985). From social support to social networks. In I. Sarason and B. Sarason (Eds.), *Social Support. Theory, Research, Applications*, 205–22. The Hague, The Netherlands: Martinus Nijhoff.

Wellman, B. and B. Leighton (1979). Networks, neighborhoods and communities. *Urban Affairs Quarterly 14*, 363–90.

White, D. R. and K. P. Reitz (1983). Graph and semigroup homomorphisms on networks of relations. *Social Networks 5*, 193–234.

White, P. A. (2008). Beliefs about interactions between factors in the natural environment a causal network study. *Applied Cognitive Psychology 22*, 559–572.

Whyte, W. F. (1998). *Street Corner Society: The Social Structure of an Italian Slum*. Chicago, IL: University of Chicago Press. First published in 1943.

Wiener, H. (1947). Structural determination of paraffin boiling points. *Journal of the American Chemical Society 69* (1), 17–20.

Windolf, P. (2006). Unternehmensverflechtung im organisierten Kapital-
ismus. Deutschland und USA im Vergleich 1896–1938. *Zeitschrift für
Unternehmensgeschichte 51*, 191–222.

Windolf, P. (2009).   Das Netzwerk der jüdischen Wirtschaftselite:
Deutschland 1914-1938. In R. Stichweh and P. Windolf (Eds.), *Inklu-
sion und Exklusion: Analysen zur Sozialstruktur und sozialen Un-
gleichheit*, 275–301. Wiesbaden, Germany: VS Verlag für Sozialwissenschaften.

Wirth, L. (1938). Urbanism as a way of life. *American Journal of Sociology 44*, 3–24.

Zachary, W. W. (1977). An information flow model for conflict and fission
in small groups. *Journal of Anthropological Research 33* (4), 452–473.

Index

Social Science